PRAISE FOR
"THE REVERSE INTERVIEW"

"Read this book if you want job offers, not job interviews."

David T. Fagan
Former CEO, Guerrilla Marketing

"As someone who used to run a publishing company, and as a 6-Time International bestselling author, I know quality when I see it. Charles' back-story is the perfect lead in to why you need to read his book if you ever want to influence someone that you have what they need. Whether you are looking for a job, or are selling a product, the same principles apply. I especially love how he took a simple concept, and reversed the thinking around it. If you are ready to stand out and get want you want, then get this book first."

Tracy Repchuk
Author, Speaker and Creator of Get a Fully Branded End to End Website Presence in Under 60 Days

"From one of the most brilliant minds in America comes an eminently readable book that will do precisely what it sets out to achieve: show you how to get stellar results. With his conversational narrative, Charles engages the reader from the start, so don't be surprised when you find you simply cannot put it down as you discover step-by-step how to realize your dreams."

Gareth Feighery
Founder, Davos Investments

"Combining the analytical skills of an engineer with his deep interest in psychology and human interaction, Charles Woolsey provides a unique, 3-step networking approach for landing a job. The process from idea to job offer is both productive and fun!"

Shoya Zichy
Author, "Personality Power and Career Match"
Creator of the five-time award-winning Color Q Personality model

"If you want to position yourself for a job in your chosen field, just do exactly what Charles recommends in his book 'The Reverse Interview'. It's the easiest way to meet the people that can launch your career. That's exactly what it did for my career."

Jason Oman
Bestselling Author, "Conversations with Millionaires", "Conversations with Female Millionaires"
Creator of Millionaire Money Formula

" 'The Reverse Interview' is an incredible resource for anyone ready to bust through the perceived barriers to achieving one's dreams. Charles leads you step by step on the journey to create the success you desire and deserve."

Virginia Barkley
No. 1 Bestselling Author, Speaker,
Organizing Strategist and Coach

"I honestly thought it was going to be another how-to-land-a-job checklist with outdated info or some 'mindset guru' nonsense void of sound strategy. When I got to the nine magic words part of the book my eyes opened as wide as the sun. I had no idea, nor did I see your solution for career advancement coming. It was one of those Quentin Tarantino out-of-nowhere moments. Simplicity and genius."

Michael Solis
Trainer, Author, Speaker

"Wow! First of all, Charles definitely thinks outside of the box. This is a fresh approach; one that I would have never thought of on my own. I think it's an excellent window of opportunity that many people just like me have never even considered. Second, the summary notes? Awesome! Just awesome! If someone (like myself) needs some encouragement or ideas for a particular topic, there they are, easy to find, without having a million bookmarks or highlights. I think this book will benefit MANY. Seriously, this is a game changer."

Kelly Toro
WISE Insurance

"If you're trying the same things over and over and not getting the results you want in your career, then read 'The Reverse Interview' and try something different! Charles Woolsey details a BOLD new approach that will open up exciting career opportunities, possibly better than you've dreamed."

Justin "Jake" Tollman
CCA Nutrient Advisors, LLC

"He's done it... a beautifully inspired book, easy to understand language that anyone can follow who wants to change their life. This book is a well-written guide that not only provides information but helps you to step out of your comfort zone and play a bigger game for yourself. Thought-provoking challenges through the exercises in this book will help you break through any blocks you might be facing. This book should be read by everyone. Having the experiences Charles has had in his life and his passion to help others not only provides credibility but also the 'why' you should pick up this book now! Find your passion and your path... the world awaits you."

Kaytlin Stead
Professional Intuitive Coach

"Throughout my career, I've zigged while others zagged and found a lot of success in an industry I love. Well, it looks like someone has let the secret out. Charles Woolsey is offering you a step-by-step plan to chart your own course by thinking outside of the proverbial box. I highly recommend it, regardless of your current position. This can open more doors than you can possibly handle in one lifetime."

Phil Ammendolia
VP Marketing, LS2 Helmets

"I commend your forward thinking and your innovative approach helping people find jobs, change careers and develop lifetime contacts while establishing their credibility in the labor force. The reverse approach gives the employee that needed edge to combat the high volume of job applicants for the limited amount of employment opportunities. Your framework is easy to follow from your story, creating the career path, writing 'the' book, follow up contacts, networking to the final system application."

Grant "Mac" McFayden
Entrepreneur, Consultant

" 'In life you can get in line or you can create your own line.' This statement is one of the foundational statements in Charles Woolsey's 'The Reverse Interview'. If conventional wisdom and thinking is what everyone is doing, then doing the opposite would seem how the achievers and successful among us accomplish what they do. 'The Reverse Interview' contains a lot of common sense but throws conventional wisdom out the window, and kudos to Charles for doing so. Based upon his years in working with and for large corporations in a variety of fields, Charles puts together a step-by-step approach to bypassing Human Resources and putting yourself in front of the true decision maker – the CEO – in a way no one else can, unless you follow Charles' process. This is a book you should read with a highlighter, but, if you don't, Charles puts a concise summary of each chapter's content before moving on to the next. A triumph for those who want to do what they love, not what they have to, 'The Reverse Interview' is just what is needed for job seekers in the 21st Century."

Dr. Eric Shoars
Author, "Triumph: Winning Big in Life with Patience, Persistence, and Perseverance"

"The best new strategy to multiply your career options I've ever seen. Whether you want to land your dream job or get promoted to the corner office, 'The Reverse Interview' will get you there."

Joey Smith
Author, Speaker, Mentor
Former CIO, The John Maxwell Company

I'm humbled...

My personal thanks to all of the people that took the time to read early copies of this book. Each and every one of you gave me the encouragement and resolve to get it finished and get it out to help those in need.

Charles Woolsey

THE REVERSE INTERVIEW

Get In, Get Hired, Get Promoted

by
CHARLES WOOLSEY

Reverse Publishing Inc.

Copyright © 2015 by Charles Woolsey

All rights reserved. No part of this book may be reproduced in any form or by any electronic or mechanical means, including information storage and retrieval systems, without written permission from the publisher.

ISBN:978-0-9909608-0-5

Cover design: Exypnos
Interior Design: Access Ideas
Editing: Donna Capodelupo, Bonnie Queen
Back cover photography: Parker Woolsey

Printed in the United States of America

CONTENTS

PREFACE

INTRODUCTION — 1

SECTION 1 - GETTING STARTED — 11
- **The Lemming Method** — 13
  The crowd is always wrong
- **Foundation** — 21
  Getting clear on what you want
- **Attention** — 37
  How to be heard, trusted and admired

SECTION 2 - THE THREE-STEP SYSTEM — 51
- **Connect** — 53
  Choose your sphere of influence
- **Collect** — 69
  To be interesting, be interested
- **Convey** — 85
  Because it's NOT who you know that matters

SECTION 3 - SYSTEM APPLICATION — 103
- **Weapons of Mass Influence** — 105
  *Human nature doesn't change,
  but you can*
- **Leverage** — 121
  *How to make (nearly) everything you do
  more effective*
- **The Big Goal** — 133
  No one can ever move your career (cheese) again

SECTION 4 - WRAP IT UP — 143

BONUS CHAPTER - SIMPLIFY AND SIMPLY GET IT DONE! — 145

ABOUT THE AUTHOR — 153

Preface

You picked up this book because you want to find a new job. Maybe you're unemployed. Or the company you work for hasn't been doing well, and you're worried about the future.

Or maybe you have a job, but it's not one you enjoy, or even like.

I know the feeling. I was once in a job that I had grown to hate. I had been promoted into a position where I was miserable. I hated what I was doing and I felt trapped.

Even worse, six people reported to me and I felt responsible for them and their futures.

One of the six clearly was not performing well. I needed to find a way to help him grow into the position, or find another, more suitable position for him.

But my boss had other ideas.

He told me to fire him, "Right now!"

"Right now" was ten days before Christmas. He was a young man with a wife and two small children, the breadwinner for his family. I was forced to fire him as he prepared to celebrate the holidays.

My boss didn't care. It had to be done immediately. No amount of discussion or compromise or alternate solutions seemed to be good enough for him.

ReverseInterview.com/bonus

So I fired him… and it broke my heart.

I felt so badly, I wanted to quit my job on the spot. But I didn't… and that broke my soul.

I had traded my integrity and my compassion for a paycheck.

To make matters worse, I was told I would be held in high regard by upper management because I had "proven" myself. To them, I showed I could make tough decisions and carry them out.

But in my mind, I had thrown that young man to the wolves, in the cold of winter, and he would have to fend for himself. I had subjected him to hardship, worries and humiliation.

I didn't quit my job. I worked there another six years. During those six years of guilt and torment, I studied human nature, marketing and positioning. I learned about motivation, influence and leadership.

And that's how this book was born.

Far too many people are out of work and desperate, or they have a job and hate it but feel trapped. Looking for a better opportunity to work where you love what you do, are appreciated for your contributions and make the kind of money you feel you need and deserve can seem like searching for a unicorn.

You're not even sure it really exists.

Even if you saw one in the distance, you would have no idea how to approach it, befriend it and make it part of your world.

Preface

This book is dedicated to making even the most elusive of opportunities attainable. It's about getting into places that seem closed and unapproachable to most job seekers.

As I was planning to write this book, my business coach asked:

"What do you want this book to accomplish?"

My response:

"I want it to help as many people as possible easily find a job in a career that they <u>really</u> love AND never be unemployed or feel trapped in a job they dislike <u>ever</u> again."

He then asked:

"Do they have to read the whole book, or is there some way you can give it to them in the first chapter? You know most people don't read the whole book, right? What can you do to help them get the results you described as fast as possible?"

Hmmm.

"What if I give them a link, not in the first chapter, but right in the preface that would give them another way to learn the core of the material in about an hour... how about that?"

"Bingo!"

Mind you, there is great value in reading the entire book. It will give you greater depth of understanding, knowledge and drive to go out and implement the "three simple steps", and it's not a huge book, but if you want or need a shortcut, here it is:

ReverseInterview.com/shortcut

Not only is there a "quick start" video there, but there are also many valuable resources that add additional depth and updates to the book.

Go ahead; take a look.

Remember…

You can do this.

Introduction

First, I want you to understand one thing…

I am NOT what you would call a "traditional" career guru.

I have not spent the last thirty years helping people write and re-write their resumes.

I have not drilled people on interviewing techniques for the past twenty years.

Nor have I examined, researched and tested the latest job boards and recruiting methods for a decade in hopes of passing on to you a slight edge over the competition.

So you may be asking yourself about now, "Why should I keep reading?"

Sometimes what you need is a small, incremental change or improvement to get where you want to go. Other times it's best to start from scratch and to rethink the situation from the beginning.

This book is about doing something completely different, not better ways of doing the same old stuff. Let's face it, if what you were already doing was working, you wouldn't be here reading this, would you?

The Reverse Interview

So if I'm not a "traditional" career guru, what is it that I can offer you?

How about a lifetime of experiences that make me uniquely qualified to look at a problem and find a new, different and better solution. That was my job for nearly thirty years. I got pretty good at it.

I patented an anti-shoplifting device that sold more than 1,000,000,000 units(that's more than one billion) over three decades (patent #4,642,640). You've likely seen it dozens or even hundreds of times at your favorite department stores.

I worked with NASA to help develop and improve experiments that were preformed aboard space shuttle missions.

I worked with medical doctors in heart, brain and lung function testing and analysis.

I have also helped rock quarries, steel mills, commercial jet designers, chicken farmers and more industries than I can list or even remember.

The only thing all these had in common was a problem that they called me in to help fix. They knew I would either help find a solution or find someone else who could.

My job function during most of that time was "Salesman" (though my actual title would change a bit). I spent nine years as a front-line salesperson averaging more than$3 million in sales each year. I then went on to hire and manage a team with the top results in a nearly $1 billion company.

Introduction

I'll give you a little hint in case you've never been in sales… people don't like to be sold. People generally don't like the thought of talking to salesmen, either.

I learned early on that while people don't like to be sold, they do like bringing in someone who will make their problems go away. I learned to never sell anyone anything… for any reason. I learned that even though my company may put the job label of "Salesman" on me, I told myself I was a problem solver and my mission was to find a way to make my customers' troubles go away.

One of my all-time favorite quotes is by Zig Ziglar (American author, salesman, and motivational speaker). He said:

"In order to have everything you want in life, all you have to do is help enough other people get what they want."

I solved a lot of problems for individuals and companies in order to help them get what they wanted. I never "sold" them anything, yet I had many, many millions of dollars in products and services purchased from me. That was my secret to being able to retire at age fifty-one.

Thanks, Zig!

I then found that retirement at some point can become meaningless. I like solving big problems. I like helping people. So I asked myself, "What big problems exist right now and how can I make a big impact in the lives of people just like you with families just like yours?"

The answer was pretty easy.

I can use what I've learned to help people get jobs!

Getting a job is a sales job. It's not only a sales job (which is the last job many people want) it's one of the toughest sales jobs imaginable because the product you are selling is YOU!

If you don't want to buy my widget, I don't take it personally. But when you don't want *me*, well, it doesn't get much more personal than that, does it?

The job market is tough. It can be VERY difficult for people of all backgrounds, experience and education levels to get anyone to notice them. For any new job posting, employers receive three hundred to four hundred resumes, on average. That's a problem for not only the applicants, but also for the companies that have to sift through the massive flood of data to try to figure out who would be the best candidate.

So the job problem is not only for you -- the applicant -- but for the company that is looking for you as well.

Your resume is adding to the burden, confusion and delay in their task of finding the perfect candidate.

Your phone call is routed to an already overflowing voicemail system.

Your online application is occupying valuable digital space on some cyber hard drive.

Your resume will most likely be entered into a database so that an intern (or maybe a software program) will scan it for keywords.

Introduction

If your resume was entered incorrectly or you missed a specific keyword, or (heaven forbid) you used a synonym, your resume will be discarded. If you made it through the first scan, your resume may make it no farther than the NEXT filter.

Typically, each resume gets about ten seconds. If you manage to pass that, then your resume may make it to the hiring manager's assistant, who will do another screen.

Even if you are the right candidate, you're lucky if the manager gets a chance to even see your resume.

And what do you hear from your end?

Perhaps a form letter from HR:

> "Thank you for your interest but..."
> "While your qualifications are impressive..."
> "We will keep your resume on file for future..."

Most likely, you will hear absolutely nothing at all.

Is it time to contact them again? Should you send another letter or email? Should you just drop in and show that you're still interested?

How often should you keep trying to get an answer before you're identified as an annoyance?

Even getting a "no" seems better than hearing nothing. At least then there is closure and you know it's time to move on.

This is the awkward and degrading cycle we get in

The Reverse Interview

when we are asking for something from someone else. It doesn't feel good for us and it doesn't feel good for them. Both parties feel uncomfortable and struggle with how to deal with it.

Here's how to avoid this whole mess.

Don't ask. Give.

Instead of bugging people and asking for things, give your time and talent. Give your attention. Find something they need and wrap it up and hand it to them like the gift that it is.

When I was in my "Salesman" mode, this was fairly straightforward. Potential clients usually knew what their issue was, and I was invited in to help solve it. I gave them my time, my knowledge and experience. They got a solution regardless of whether it was something they could buy from me. They knew I was there to help them. Therefore, they never hesitated to call me in again because my intentions were sincere. Relationships like this, in the long run, result in many more purchases than when you walk in with the goal of selling something.

In the "get a job" role, things get a little trickier.

And things get a little easier.

Instead of solving a unique problem or issue at each company the way that I had to, I have devised a plan for you to go in and give them something that they desperately want but can't easily do for themselves. It's something that they would gladly give their time, talent and energy for. They will welcome you with open arms.

Introduction

You don't walk in and ask for a job.

You don't try to convince them how great you are and how much value you can add to their company.

You won't have to keep following up and risk irritating them and discouraging yourself.

You won't need to do anything that makes it look like you are there simply for your own benefit.

Whenever someone suspects that you are there for personal gain, they question everything you do or say. They're looking for what your angle is. They analyze every word that comes out of your mouth looking for exaggeration and trickery.

OK, so now you're asking yourself, *"How can I walk into any company and get the full attention of any person there* and if I could, *how valuable for my career and my future would that skill be?"*

Here's a clue: What if a local television reporter called ACME Widget Inc. and said a producer wanted to air a story about how ACME had become so successful over the five years it's been in business? What if this story would be seen by thousands of people around the country? What if all this publicity was going to be one hundred percent free?

Would the person who answered the phone at ACME Widget Inc. try his/her best to find the right person to connect the reporter to? Don't you think everyone at ACME Widget Inc. would be ready to jump into action if they could help with the story?

I'm not sure how to say "Heck Yes!" loudly enough in print.

They would be all over it.

You can get a similar response without working at a TV station.

You can do it with no deception, in absolute integrity, and it will benefit the company and your career every single time.

You can create a career path on your own terms.

You don't have to be waiting and hoping and praying that something good will happen if only someone else would just see your value. If only someone would give you a chance.

You can create your own chances.

Here is the key to getting the most out of the book and out of this process.

"Winners" will read this book and ask themselves, "How can I make this information work for ME"?

I hate to say it, and it sounds harsh, but "losers" will read this same book and say to themselves, "This will never work for me because (*fill in your lame excuse here*)."

The quality of your outcome and the quality of your life is determined by the quality of the questions you ask.

Expect positive outcomes.

Ask good, empowering questions.

Be a winner.

SUMMARY NOTES:

1. The author is NOT a "traditional" career guru who rehashes the same old advice; he is a problem solver.
2. The author has over thirty years' experience solving problems ranging from shoplifting, NASA missions and medical issues to chicken farming and manufacturing steel.
3. While people don't like being "sold," they do like having their problems solved.
4. The problem for most job-seekers is their inability to gain the attention of the right people.
5. Solve a problem to gain rapport.
6. Use the tactics of a TV reporter.
7. Be a winner.
8. Ask yourself how you can make this information work for you.

Section 1
GETTING STARTED

THE LEMMING METHOD
The crowd is always wrong

"In fact, the only way to get ahead is to find errors in conventional wisdom."

Larry Ellison
CEO, Oracle

I think everyone knows the story of the lemmings and running with the crowd, even when that means running off the cliff to your peril. The lemming story is used to illustrate the obvious problems associated with blindly following the pack. Most of us would never be so foolish as to run off a cliff, or to do anything else that would hurt us or waste our valuable time and efforts.

Or would we?

You see, there is a built-in programming function that we human beings have. It's to observe others and use that input to take shortcuts in our decision making process. I'll talk more regarding this in a later chapter about the work of Dr. Robert Cialdini. For now, just understand that following others is part of human nature. It's one way that we make choices. Going against those "automatic mode" impulses requires a conscious effort.

ReverseInterview.com/bonus

Here is an example from when I was in college. It was 1979and due to the Iranian Revolution, gasoline was getting scarce. The prices were going up, and people were scared. Everyone felt the need to keep a full tank at all times "just in case" they needed it. Since gas was hard to get, they wanted it even more.

Many gas stations were out of gasoline completely. Those that did have gas usually had very long lines. And what happened when people saw those long lines? They got in them. Why? Because they assumed that the stations with the long lines had gas. Who would go to a station with no gas?

Right next door to the station with the long lines was often a station with no line at all. The assumption was that if there was no line, there must be no gas, right? Sometimes that assumption was right, but sometimes it was wrong. Those willing to drive to the deserted gas stations and at least ask about availability were often rewarded with all the gas they needed with zero wait time.

Here's another example. My son's high school graduation ceremony was at a nearby college. We parked more than a quarter mile away and started walking across campus. Once we got about a block away, we could see the line forming to get into the auditorium. When we got closer, we saw that hundreds of people were in a single line that had started to circle the building.

I'm embarrassed to say, but I was heading for the end of that line when my wife looked at the entrance to the building as we got a little nearer (I would love to say that it was me and my superior observation skills

… but no). She noticed that there were two entrances, one of them with only about a dozen people in line. By the time we got to the short line, there was no wait at all. We walked right in and claimed our seats. We sat in padded and air-conditioned comfort while hundreds of parents and family members stood outside sweating in that increasingly long line in the hot, Atlanta sun.

What does this have to do with getting a job?

Well, the "job hunting system" that snares most job seekers is set up to put candidates in lines… long, long lines full of hopeful people of varying backgrounds, desires and capabilities each anticipating a chance at the prize: an interview with just about anyone who will listen.

Job seekers with even basic research skills will find these lines in lots of places: online job boards, advertised job openings at specific companies, job fairs, listings on Craigslist, local newspapers, and social media (LinkedIn, Facebook, etc.).

It's easy to find a line and get in it. It feels safe and comfortable to be surrounded by other people. You may not get the job, but there are lots of other people not getting the job too, so it feels okay. You're in good company; it's not your fault.

If getting into a certain line isn't working, maybe the answer is just to get in more lines. It's a little like buying lottery tickets. If you buy just one your odds aren't very good, but if you buy two, your odds just doubled! Why not buy ten or one hundred or as many as you can afford?

That's what people do with getting into lines for jobs. They get into as many as they can afford. Since most lines are free, why not get into every one you can find?

Unfortunately, there *is* a cost to getting into these lines. There may not be a monetary fee, but there is a cost in time and effort and, more importantly, a cost in confidence and self-esteem and optimism.

Every line that you get into that doesn't lead anywhere takes a toll. It takes away a little piece of you. Little by little the unsuccessful job seeker feels smaller, less wanted and less confident. I believe this is a major reason millions of people have given up even trying to find a job.

Knowing that people are giving up on their hopes and dreams is the part that I find really gut wrenching.

There's a saying that you don't fail at anything until you give up. When a job seeker plays a game that has so few winners, giving up is a natural response. Some people keep pushing forward, but many more don't. Either way, the game takes its toll.

There *is* another way.

Just as at the graduation ceremony, there could be other doors that open wide for you. Doors where there is no waiting. Doors that lead directly to your desired destination. Doors that YOU can choose right now, today, instead of waiting on life's lottery to choose you.

I'm going to warn you, though.

It just may require you to get a little bit

uncomfortable.

There is a reason those gas pumps had no customers even though they were full of gas. Someone had to put himself "out there" to go see why no one was using them. There was a chance that the pump was empty, and he would look silly going to that station.

Going up to that pump could be a little uncomfortable for a LOT of people. It seems safer, easier and more comfortable just to get in the line. Getting in line with everyone else is a lemming tactic. Even if it is the wrong thing to do, no one is looking at you and judging you for being a little bit different.

Are you willing to get a little bit uncomfortable?

Seriously. I'm asking you this question.

Here is something I learned from my mentor, T. Harv Eker (author, businessman and motivational speaker known for his theories on wealth and motivation):

Everything you want is outside of your comfort zone, otherwise you'd already have it.

Think about it. Was it a huge leap to check out that gas pump? I don't think so, but most people wouldn't do it. And because they wouldn't do it they ended up at the back of the line instead of heading out to the beach (metaphorically speaking) with a full tank of gas.

The crowd gets into the line because it's comfortable. It's a shortcut to making their own informed decisions and it's what everyone else is doing. There's very little risk of standing out or being noticed.

Simple changes can have dramatically different results.

Get in line vs. start your own line.

Do you want to be a lemming or do you want to be the self-aware captain of your destiny?

The choice is always yours.

In this book, you will learn how to start your own line directly to what you want in your career.

This book is not only to encourage you to chart your own course, but to give you a simple system to be successful now and throughout your career journey.

Summary Notes:

1. Don't be a lemming and just follow the crowd.
2. If there is something that you want, don't just jump into the first line you see.
3. There is almost always a shortcut or a shorter line.
4. Doing more of a bad plan is not a good plan.
5. Everything you want is outside of your comfort zone.
6. Be willing to do what is uncomfortable in the short run so you can have what you want in the long run.
7. Make your own choices.
8. Create your own line.

The Reverse Interview

FOUNDATION
Getting clear on what you want

"Famous archer Howard Hill won all 267 archery contests he entered. He could hit a bull's-eye at 50 feet then split that arrow with the next. Would it be possible for you to shoot more accurately than him? YES, if he was blindfolded and spun around."

Zig Ziglar
American author, salesman and motivational speaker

This very well could be the most important chapter in the book. For those of you who are willing to think, explore and further define what it is you want to do, keep reading very closely.

It sets the tone for those who are serious.

I can show you how to get the job you want. The problem is, most people don't know what they truly want.

Showing you how to get a job, a really good job, is easy. I want more for you than that. I want you to have not only a really good job, but a really good job that makes you happy.

… A job that makes you want to get up in the morning.

… A job that makes Friday just another day.

… A job that makes you feel good about whatever it is that matters to you.

And of course, a job that pays you really well.

Are you sure that you know what job you want?

If so, that's great! Just skim this chapter and fill in the sections at the end about your ideal job and why it matters to you. This information will be needed later in the book

The good news?

You can always change your mind. It's quick and easy to implement the strategies in this book more than once and with more than one career choice. In fact, I encourage you to do this any time you want to explore other employment possibilities. There is no better way to get to the essence of a career choice than by using what you are about to learn.

Let's get started in the discovery process!

First of all, you need to understand that this book and the strategies inside are based upon the understanding that you want a fulfilling and rewarding and interesting and inspiring job or career or vocation or whatever you want to call it.

Agreed?

Therefore, you need to have something you care about. You have to be willing to put energy into learning about it and being the best that you can be at doing it.

Attitude is everything.

Many an otherwise "less than perfect" employee has excelled at her career simply because she had a great attitude. Likewise, many an otherwise "stellar" employee has been fired for no other reason than her poor attitude.

Sir Richard Branson (founder of the Virgin Group, which includes Virgin Air, Virgin Mobile and more than four hundred other companies) says that the single most important trait to look for is attitude.

In my opinion, the best way to have a good attitude about anything is for it to be something you care about, something you have a passion for and something you can pour yourself into.

Therefore, there is no better place to start looking for what you want to do with your career than to figure out what it is that you care about.

I'm going to help you find what you care about and what work you should be doing. There have been many books written on this one topic alone. You're getting it here as an extra benefit.

Don't take this lightly.

It's important, and it's been distilled from many other sources all in one nice, neat and concise exercise.

Answer these questions to get on a track that will serve you long-term.

Write your answers on another sheet of paper, or download this form that you can print out here:

ReverseInterview.com/bonus

Take your time and be thorough. An extra hour spent here can save you years of frustration later.

Formal Education

1. What formal education do you have?
2. What have you studied?
3. What have you learned from, or because of, this education?
4. Is there anything you would have done differently?
5. What advice would you give others who are thinking about going down this path?

Informal Education

1. What topic have you read three or more books about?
2. What seminars have you attended?
3. What would your friends say that you're an expert in (hint: ask them)?
4. What topics do friends and family seek your advice on?
5. Where have you traveled?
6. What capabilities do you possess that are different from most other people's?

Ambitions

1. If salary was not a consideration, what would you do for a living?
2. What is on your bucket list of things you'd like to do?
3. What did you dream of doing when you were a child?
4. What would you like to be remembered for long after you're gone?
5. What would you do if you knew you wouldn't fail?

Accomplishments

1. Name the five most important accomplishments of your life so far (either personally or professionally).
2. What were some of the most difficult things that you've overcome?
3. Where in your life do you see yourself as an overachiever, doing things that seem improbable given your background and resources?
4. When did you feel the most proud?
5. What would your closest friends and family say about you and what you've done?
6. If you were to write your autobiography, what would the chapter titles be?

Competencies

1. List at least twenty things that you consider yourself to be good, very good, or excellent at doing.

2. Next to each item, list the approximate number of hours you have spent over your lifetime doing that task or activity.
3. Again, next to each item on the list, rank it from zero to five, with five being the highest according to how much pleasure you feel when engaged in this activity.
4. Look for overlap with what you are really good at, how much time you've spent doing it and how much pleasure you get from doing it.

Experience

1. List all the full-time and part-time jobs you've had.
2. What did you enjoy most at each of them?
3. What did you enjoy least?
4. What would a day at your ideal job look like?
5. How much money would you make per year at your ideal job?
6. What jobs do your friends or family have that you are envious of?
7. What do you willingly volunteer your time for?

Compiling the Results

Go over your responses to all the questions.

Do you see any overlap?

Do you see any recurring themes?

Take your time and ponder this for a while. This is not a sprint. You didn't get where you are in five minutes, so don't be too hard on yourself for not having an immediate "ah ha" moment here.

Let me share a personal note ...

I kept looking for the "one thing" that would be the end-all theme or career for the rest of my life.

I didn't know what it was, and I was scared to death that I would pick the wrong thing, whatever that one thing was.

Here's what I found out:

First of all, there may not be that "one thing," and that's okay. What's important is to pick something that matters to you today.

It may change later, and that's okay too.

You can always apply yourself to something different tomorrow, but don't worry about that right now.

The other thing that I realized was that the "one thing" may not look like you expected it to.

You might be thinking about being a CPA, or a marketing person or even a rock and roll star.

But what your heart is really telling you is that you may like working with numbers in relative solitude or that you enjoy figuring out how to influence other people's decision making or that you crave being the center of attention and have a need for creativity.

Once you look at the reasons behind a possible career choice, it can open other ideas about where those desires could also be used.

I highly recommend getting the book "Strengths

Finder 2.0" by Tom Rath and the Gallup organization. I say this partly for the information you'll find in the book, but mostly because of the strengths finder quiz that you will have access to.

The quiz will rank your top five strengths out of thirty-four possible areas that the authors have identified.

It is especially interesting and liberating when you learn how to apply those strengths to possible career decisions.

It's your natural strengths that provide your drive and enthusiasm toward tasks and the feeling of fulfillment in your work, play and everything that you do.

Whenever I managed a team of people, I had each person take this quiz and give me their scores so that I could see what their strengths were. This helped me manage them because I could steer them in the directions where they would be more effective *and happier.*

The Results?

My team performed better than any other team in an $800 million per year organization.

I'd say it worked … for three reasons.

First, I could talk to them in the terms that they most cared about and focus their energies into the right directions.

Second, everyone who was in the right position could remain motivated because they were doing mostly what they loved and very little of what drained them.

Third, it helped me identify those who were not in the right positions.

After reading one young lady's strengths, I invited her to dinner so that we could discuss them. I told her I was having trouble understanding how she could be happy and fulfilled in her current position based on the results of the quiz. I just couldn't see how she could get her job done while maximizing her time playing to her strengths and minimize all the other tasks that would sap her energy.

After I told her of my concerns, she started to cry.

She told me that she wasn't happy at all.

It was a shock to me because she was doing a good job. Not an outstanding job like I was hoping I could coach her into, but she was performing well.

She turned in her resignation two weeks later. She realized her current job would never be fulfilling. She went on to do some technical writing and programming that she loved. Now that she was happy again, she reconnected with her college sweetheart and got married.

There's an important key in this story. It is quite possible to perform well in a position that you don't like. The problem is that it will take its toll on you eventually, in more areas of your life than just your job. It most surely will affect your personal life too.

Back to the questions in this book…

Go over your responses to the questions again, but this time also think about the results of your strengths finder quiz (or what you already know about what you naturally enjoy doing). See where you can apply your best qualities, experience, training, ambition and education to a career that you will find rewarding.

Remember that you can always change your career choice any time you decide that you want to. In fact, the process you are learning now is a great way to try things that you think you might like. If you do like your choice, then continue to pursue it. If not, just try another route.

As you work through the steps in Section 2, it will become crystal clear to you if you are following the right path. It will also become painfully clear if you have chosen the wrong one.

That is the beauty of this system: the feedback you will get along the way.

Just trust me and follow the process, okay?

Great!

Here are the final two steps for this chapter and the ones that will set the stage for the next section.

Career: Write down what career you would like to go after.

Why: Write down specifically why it matters to you.

Career Examples and Why

Career: CPA.
Why: Because I want to help small businesses grow and succeed.

Career: Electrical Engineer.
Why: Because I like finding more efficient design methods.

Career: Real Estate.
Why: Because I love finding the perfect home for people no matter what their needs are.

Career: Retail Sales.
Why: Because I love meeting new people and instantly gaining a connection with them.

Career: Mediator.
Why: Because I love finding common ground and areas of agreement.

Are you getting the idea?

Good!

Experiment with different ideas until you find something that resonates with you, something that not only feels comfortable, but also that excites you. The bigger the excited feeling you get, the bigger and more positive your results are going to be later.

Are you still having trouble coming up with the "one thing" that you want to work on?

Here's another one of the tricks that I learned as a

teenager trying to make my first BIG decisions.

First step- If you have a choice of two or three things but you're not sure which is right, just make a decision. Pick any one of the alternatives, then go through this simple process:

- Sit in a quiet, comfortable room.
- Relax.
- Take three deep breaths and close your eyes.
- Relax your body and clear your mind.
- Imagine yourself in that role you chose.
- What does it look like when you get to where you work?
- What do your surroundings look like?
- Who will you see around you?
- Are they happy?
- Do you feel energized?
- Can you see yourself here every day?
- What tasks will you be doing?
- Are you looking forward to the end of the day?
- Do everything you can think of to put yourself in that situation and analyze your reaction to it.
- Sleep on it.
- Ask yourself the next morning how you feel. Do you feel at ease? Do you feel excited? Do you feel scared, trapped or miserable? *These are your clues.*

Next step- One at a time, pick each of the other alternatives. Go through the same process. Contemplate each decision and live with it for however long it takes to feel the consequences and your reactions to your choice.

One option will feel better than the others.

One choice will have you feeling excited and maybe a little bit scared, but for a good reason. Good choices that expand you can and should be at least a little bit scary.

This works every time for me. If there is no clear winner, then alter the choices that you made or tune them a little to create the most fulfilling choices that you can.

Again, the choice you make can be changed, and it will reveal itself when you start applying the steps in the next section.

Once you have made your decisions about what it is you want to do and why you want do it, it's time for celebration. You have just completed the most important, and perhaps the most difficult, part of your job search.

Now that you have a target, it's just a matter of perfecting your aim.

SUMMARY NOTES:

1. To get what you want, you must know what you want.
2. Getting a great job is easy if you know what you want.
3. Pick something you want to do; it can always be changed later.
4. Attitude is everything; it's the single most important trait.
5. To have a great attitude, find something that you are passionate about.
6. Take the quiz in "Strengths Finder 2.0" by Tom Rath to find what you naturally do best.
7. Go through a discovery process to find what you care about most.
8. Compile your answers and look for patterns.
9. Come up with your "why" for that job.
10. If you are still having trouble deciding, make a choice and sleep on it.

ATTENTION
How to be heard, trusted and admired

"To be trusted is a greater compliment than being loved."

George MacDonald
Scottish author, poet, and Christian minister

It's a very noisy world out there. Seth Godin is one of my favorite marketers, and he writes about this quite frequently.

The world is full of people all yelling, "Look at me! See how great I am? Wouldn't you like to learn more about me?"

When everyone is parading, writing or screaming, "Look at me," it all sounds the same; it all runs together and ultimately none of it is heard.

Godin wrote a book called "Purple Cow" and the first issues of the book were actually packaged inside of a cardboard milk carton designed to look like a purple cow.

"Purple Cow" is about being different, being outstanding and being noticed.

The Reverse Interview

Take a ride through the rural countryside and you will not be surprised to see cows … hundreds, maybe thousands of cows. Eventually you may see so many cows that you stop noticing them at all.

But a purple cow?

If you saw one, not only would you notice it but you would almost surely stop your car, take pictures, tell all your friends about it and even post the pictures to your favorite social media site.

Purple cows are remarkable (worth talking about) because they are unique, cut through the noise and stand out in a world of sameness.

Much of what I read in dozens of books and articles about standing out and getting a job in today's job market is about how to get a bigger megaphone. It's about how to be louder than everyone else and cut through the noise by sheer volume. That's obviously not exactly what they say, but that is *in effect* what they are suggesting as a solution.

That's what I would call a quantity tactic vs. a quality strategy. It may work if being loud and obnoxious is who you really are (as you annoy a hundred times as many people as you attract), but is that the way you want to be known?

Is raising the noise level in your industry the best solution to being seen as a desirable player?

A qualifying question I ask myself in these situations is "if everyone did this, would the world (or my industry) be a better place?" If the answer is "no," then I try hard to steer away from it and find a better,

Attention

more sensible solution.

In most circumstances, being louder is not better.

The purple cow isn't louder.

The purple cow is standing in the field like every other cow, but somehow it manages to draw you in.

It's attracting attention by being what it is and allowing you to form your own opinion about its presence.

It's encouraging you to go out and tell the world that it exists.

Perhaps there is someone out there who always has wanted a purple cow. Perhaps there is someone out there who didn't know a purple cow existed. But now it's on her "must have" list.

She's got to get it.

Now.

At any cost.

There is great power in being different and attractive in a low key, low volume way.

Yell in a room full of people and they will back up and cut you off.

Whisper and they will lean in, pay attention and remember what you said.

Let me give a few examples of whispering and getting people to lean in, in a figurative sense. In this case, I'm talking about getting people to notice and pay attention to you.

Years ago, when I was leading a small sales team, I would occasionally need to hire a new person. At this particular time, I was not in need of an additional team member, but someone within the company contacted me and asked to meet with me about a future position in my group.

Normally, this would have been a nonstarter because I didn't need anyone at that time.

But this case was different. He said he didn't want the position right now; he just wanted to learn more about what the position was about and what I would be looking for in an ideal candidate once I was looking for one again.

So, we scheduled the meeting.

And we talked.

Or, more accurately, I talked about ninety-five percent of the time, which is the opposite of what I normally do.

After the forty-five minutes or so we had together, I wanted to hire him even though I didn't have a spot open.

Why?

What happened?

It took me some time to figure it out... a LOT of time. I didn't have the experience and the tools to put the pieces together and answer that question for several more years. Reading, learning and using the irrefutable laws of influence and marketing helped me to not only figure it out, but to put together a system for you to easily replicate the outcome.

Actively listening to someone makes that person feel interesting and important. We all appreciate someone who makes us feel like that.

I remember reading an article years ago about the "Most Trusted Man in the World". I think it was in the 1980s. Any guess as to who that might have been?

Walter Cronkite.

For those of you too young to remember, Walter Cronkite was a news anchorman. His job was to report on the news and frequently that meant interviewing people. He would talk with a huge variety of people from the Average Joe on the streets to world leaders from around the globe.

What was his training?

What were his qualifications for becoming the most trusted man in the world?

He seemed likeable, and he was associated with big names and average people ... that's pretty much it as far as I know.

I got curious a couple years ago and Googled the "Most Trusted Woman in the World". The person whose name overwhelmingly came up in the search over and over was ...

Oprah Winfrey.

It's much more likely that you've heard of Oprah,

The Reverse Interview

unless you've been secluded in the far reaches of … I can't even think of where that might be. Everyone has heard of her.

What did Oprah do?

She associated herself with lots of average and well-known people.

She's known for:

- Being a parenting expert, though she has no children of her own
- Being a marriage expert, though she's never been married
- Being a diet expert, though she's spent most of her life trying to lose weight, mostly unsuccessfully

Now I'm not saying she has no other talents or that she hasn't done a lot to put herself in the position she enjoys, but the primary thing that put her over the top was the people she has been seen with and the topics she discussed with them.

You have talents too … quite likely you have even more talents and abilities than Oprah or Walter.

In the '80s there was a huge movement in the real estate market called Other People's Money (OPM). It was all about how to leverage the financial assets of other people to invest and make money in real estate.

I call the Oprah and Walter phenomena Other People's Authority (OPA). It's about leveraging the reputation and reach of other people to further your own goals.

Attention

On to the next topic.

Think about your first love interest. You know ... the first one who really got your heart tied up in a knot. Maybe the one who "got away." The one who still occupies a very special place in your heart. Maybe the one you're still with today.

Now think about the movies you saw together, the places you went and the popular music of the day. When you hear that song or see that movie or go to that special place, you are transported back in time to that first love.

When you are in a highly emotional state, you automatically associate the things around you with that emotional state.

You can't help it and neither can I (or anyone else, for that matter). It's just how we are wired.

It's very powerful stuff we're talking about here!

Imagine being able to get associated, in a very positive way, with influential people and their most impactful experiences ... the ones that tie you in with their greatest accomplishments.

Okay, let's summarize the essential points in this chapter so far:

1. Cut through all the noise.
2. Be different.
3. Get people to "lean in."
4. Listen more than you talk.
5. Leverage OPA (Other People's Authority).
6. Get yourself associated with positive feelings.

ReverseInterview.com/bonus

There is one simple way that you can accomplish all of these goals and put yourself in position to get an interview in any profession you want.

Write a book

Wait. Did he say write a book?

Yes! I said *write a book!*

Sound too difficult? Let me make it simple.

Have the top experts in your field write a book for you.

Instead of plastering the earth with copies of your resume in hopes of finding a job, why not ask the top people at the top companies that you'd like to work for to sit down for an interview.

Not just any interview, but a "Reverse Interview" where you get to ask the questions. The person asking the questions is in control and not in the hot seat. The person in control will be you. You get to pick all the questions and your guest expert is in the hot seat, ready to answer them.

Here's why writing an interview-style book is the perfect way to get noticed in your field, and how it applies to what you've already learned:

1. Cut through all the noise:

    You cut through all of the noise by giving the gift of these experts being appreciated in your book. You are paying it forward. You are honoring their experience and knowledge.

2. Be different:

    You are different because you are demonstrating how much you care about your profession and the people who have made their mark in it. You are taking the initiative. Who else do you think is doing this? Answer: Virtually no one!

3. Get people to "lean in:"

    Your quiet, calm approach will have them "leaning in" to learn more about how they can contribute to your project. Your "giving" nature will have them wanting to know more about you and what makes you tick.

4. Listen more than you talk:

    You will listen to them talk about the subject they care so much about and their story associated with it. You will only need to moderate and steer the conversation. People love people who listen ... it's a very rare trait but so easy to do.

5. Leverage OPA (Other People's Authority):

    The most efficient way to move up the ladder of credibility and authority in your profession is to be associated with the people who are already there. Just do what Oprah and Walter did. Talk to prominent people that can enhance your standing and reputation.

6. Get yourself associated with positive feelings:

The Reverse Interview

> Asking the right questions will get your expert to re-live and remember all the positive emotions they went through to get where they are now. Get them to relive their greatest triumphs, and those positive feelings will be transferred to you.

Most people are competing for the twenty percent of job openings that are actually advertised.

Eighty percent of jobs are not advertised. They go to the people who already have an "in." These are the people the hiring managers already know, have some kind of relationship with or are connected to.

After you finish your book, these are the benefits you will enjoy:

You will be connected with key people.

You will have relationships with industry leaders.

You will be associated with top people and their best feelings.

Now *you* are in the running for that eighty percent of jobs that you didn't have access to before. This one thing alone gives you five times the chance not only to get a job, but to get one of the best jobs that are never advertised.

About those eighty percent jobs ...

They're the ones that are easy to fill because they're fun, interesting, pay the best and aren't talked about until they're gone.

With each person you interview, your connections,

credibility and authority get wider, deeper and stronger.

That is what that candidate did with me years ago. I talked, he listened and I came away with the feeling of how great he was. It seemed strange at the time, but now I know the reasons why it worked and I know how to repeat it.

There are three steps to making this system work and each has its own chapter in Section 2. They are:

Step 1

Connect with key people in positions of power, authority and influence to build your network of potential employers. These are the people you would otherwise have zero chance of meeting. (Build your network.)

Step 2

Collect expert wisdom, strategies, challenges, insights and methods from these contacts to bypass failure and to uncover the shortcuts to success in your desired career. (Interview experts and record what they say.)

Step 3

Convey your message, commitment, credibility and your authority everywhere (online and offline). Inform and inspire while initiating employment opportunities. (Transcribe your interviews into a book.)

In case you're thinking "that's not a 'real' book if I just transcribe the conversations with other people," I suggest that you think again.

The best-selling book series in the history of (non-Bible) books is the "Chicken Soup" series with hundreds of titles, millions and millions of books in print and more than $1 billion in sales.

Here are just a few examples of the books in the series:

Chicken Soup for the Soul
Chicken Soup for the Pre-Teen Soul
Chicken Soup for the Couples Soul
Chicken Soup for the Dog Lover's Soul
Chicken Soup for the Soul Love Stories
Chicken Soup for the Grieving Soul
Chicken Soup for the Prisoner's Soul

Just about every soul imaginable has its own "Chicken Soup" book!

These books are just compilations of other people's stories.

Now, I am NOT suggesting that you will make a billion dollars with your book or that you will become the most trusted person in America. But I AM suggesting that you can very easily achieve a small portion of what the "Chicken Soup" series has done.

You will connect with enough of the right people to have a job or career that you thoroughly enjoy, to secure your financial future and potentially to go on to live a very happy and fulfilled life.

SUMMARY NOTES:

1. It's a noisy world.
2. Shouting about how great you are only adds to the noise.
3. Find a way to stand out quietly, like a purple cow does.
4. Yell and people will back up.
5. Whisper and people will lean in and listen.
6. The most trusted man and woman in America became trusted and famous by being associated with other famous people; their fame came from being around the famous.
7. Learn how to use OPA (Other People's Authority) to attain your goals.
8. When you are in a highly emotional state, you automatically associate the things around you with that emotional state.
9. Have experts in your field write your book for you.
10. On average, only twenty percent of jobs are advertised.
11. Using what you learn in this book will give you access to the unadvertised jobs.
12. The next chapters go into the three steps of completing your book: Connect, Collect and Convey.

Section 2
THE THREE-STEP SYSTEM

CONNECT
Choose your sphere of influence

"The greatest ability in business is to get along with others and to influence their actions."

John Hancock
Merchant, statesman, and prominent
Patriot of the American Revolution

Fill in the blank ... "It's not what you know, it's _____ you know."

I think most people would say, "It's <u>who</u> you know," and that may be true for some situations.

In this case, I think it should read like this: "It's not what you know, but who knows YOU."

I'm sure Oprah and Walter know a lot of people, but what gives them their reach, influence and power are the people who know them. The millions upon millions of people who know them.

Apple became the highest-valued company in the world because of the number of people who know and buy its products. I don't think it's because of the number of people that Steve Jobs knew personally.

So, let's find the people in your industry who will possess the potential to have the biggest impact on your career, entice them into your sphere of influence and interview them for your book.

Why?

Because there are a LOT of people who know them. If you become associated with them, you can reach into their sphere of influence too.

By reaching out to just a few key people, your circle of influence grows exponentially.

I don't believe there is a more powerful force for moving your career forward than leveraging other people for their knowledge, experience and influence.

Get prepared for what will happen

If you contact a well-connected person and ask for an interview for your book, the first thing he's going to ask is, "What is the name of your book, and what is it about?"

Wouldn't it be a great idea to have a great book title all ready?

Let's get a working title for your book.

Remember what you wrote in the earlier chapter about what you want to do and why? If not, go back and read what you wrote in that section. That's the core message for your title and for your subtitle.

Remember the list I offered to get you started? Here are the examples I gave and how you can turn them into book titles.

Career: CPA.

Why: Because I want to help small businesses grow and succeed.

Possible title and subtitle:

Choosing the right CPA

Your business edge to being competitive in any market

Career: Electrical Engineer.

Why: Because I like finding more efficient design methods.

Possible title and subtitle:

The Engineer's Code

Getting more done with less effort

Career: Real Estate.

Why: Because I love finding the perfect home for people no matter what their needs are.

Possible title and subtitle:

Where the Heart Is

Fifteen steps to make sure you have the home of your dreams

Career: Retail Sales.

Why: Because I love meeting new people, instantly

gaining a connection with them and helping them find what they need.

Possible title and subtitle:

Brick and Mortar

Online sites can never compete with a live person who cares

Career: Mediator.

Why: Because I love finding common ground and areas of agreement and avoiding legal hassles.

Possible title and subtitle:

Mediation

Both parties win and the lawyers get nothing

These may not be the perfect titles for you, but they demonstrate a principle. Use your career field as the basis for the title (feel free to play with the meanings of words) and your "why" becomes the basis for the subtitle. The subtitle gets into the finer details, the specific things that you are interested in and what you will interview your experts about.

An even more impactful subtitle that helps you get interviews might include a reference to your expert interviewees.

Examples of subtitles that feature your experts:

"As told by the top Chicago CPA firms"

"From 10 of the most respected engineering minds"

"Strategies of 7 home happiness specialists"

"By the people who make offline shopping fun"

"From the experts who create win-win outcomes"

Featuring your experts in the subtitle gives them even more reason and enticement to be involved in your project with you.

You can also find title ideas by looking at other books in your area of interest. Search on Amazon or Barnes and Noble for books and titles for inspiration.

Think about calling your experts, and imagine telling them the title of your book. Will it make your call easier? Are you not only comfortable but excited to talk about your book?

Keep working until you are excited to tell the world about the great book you are writing. If you are passionate about your book, it's much easier to get others interested in working with you.

A word about vision ...

Want to make it even easier to become motivated and to get your prospective expert interviewees excited to work with you? It's always easier if you and they can see the end product.

It's why architects build scale models to show their clients. If you can see a likeness of the end product, it compels you to make it a reality.

This is the perfect time to make a virtual copy of your book ... the outside of it, anyway. Create a digital 3D image of your book that you can see and show to others. Print it, and put in on your bathroom mirror and on your computer monitor.

There are lots of ways to create a 3D model of your book, but for now, I'll give you the quickest, easiest, cheapest way:

Fiverr.com

That's not a typo (yes, two r's). The creative people on this site, for about $5, will do lots of incredible things for you. It's worth a little time to look around.

Fiverr.com (Home page changes frequently)

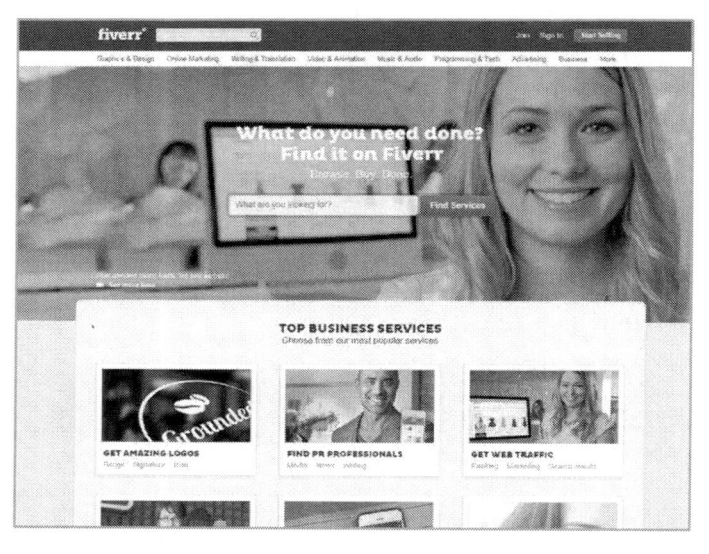

It's a great way to get a 3D digital version of your book. Search Fiverr for "eBook cover" and you'll see plenty of people ready to make your book cover jump out and grab you and your experts.

Here is an example of a search for "eBook Cover"

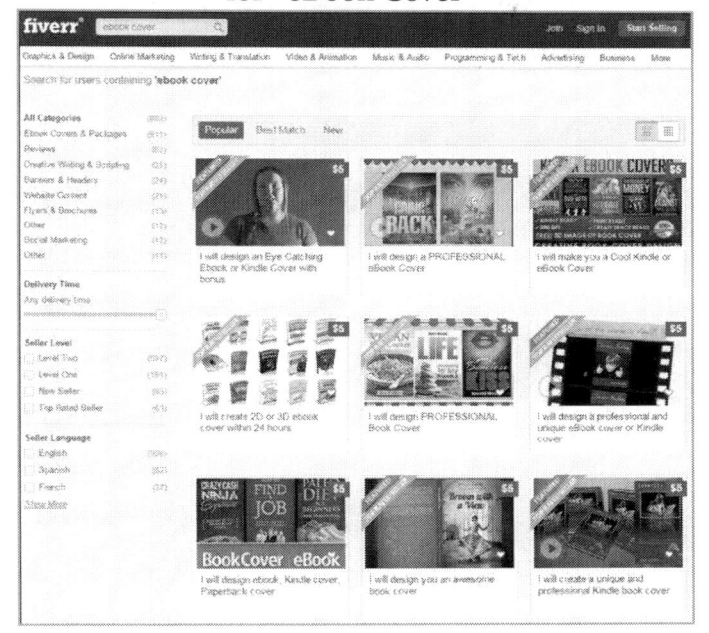

Simply pick a designer whose work you like, give the title and subtitle of your book, and give some direction about the colors and look you'd like. Choose something they've done before or give some examples from Amazon for them to model.

Voilà!

In a couple of days you'll have something to show and something to work toward. Put the image at the bottom of your emails to prospective interviewees. You can also have a flat (2D) version made, print it, and wrap it around another book to simulate a hard copy of your book too!

Next step?

Now you're ready to find the experts that you want to interview. You have your field, you have your "why" and you have the book title, subtitle and 3D picture to show the work that they'll be contributing to!

> *Side Note:*
>
> Remember, anyone can hire a "warm body," a robot, a person to fill a seat ... but what is really needed, hard to find and worth more than a paycheck is someone who cares, is motivated to learn and wants to be the best at what he does.
>
> The fact that you are working on your book shows an industry leader that you are in the top 0.1 percent of everyone out there. Think about that, and know you are doing the best thing possible for your career as you interview people for your book.

Make a list of all the potential companies where you could find someone to interview for your book. You should have a short list of the really big players in your industry *and* you should have a longer list of the companies that you might want to work with.

Why two lists?

The big players are the ones most everyone in your field has heard of. You've chosen them for name recognition and credibility. If you have trouble convincing anyone to agree to an interview, drop some of the big names. Mention that they are on your list to be interviewed too. Your potential interviewees

Reverse Interview
"Quick Start" Certificate

For a limited time purchasers of this book may have access to additional video training

Visit:
ReverseInterview.com/special
Or Scan this QR Code:

The Reverse Interview

will take you more seriously and will want to be associated with those other big names.

The second list is your real target: companies that you'd like to work for. Of course, there may be some overlap between the two lists, and that's okay.

Aim for a total list of at least ten to twenty companies, but feel free to add as many as you'd like.

If you're having trouble finding your target companies, go to Google and enter search terms such as:

1. Top CPA firms in USA
2. Best engineering companies to work for
3. Real estate brokers in San Francisco

Putting a city into the search will help you narrow the list by geographic area. This is most important if you want to talk with companies in a specific location where you'd like to live.

You can also look in trade magazines or lists of attendees at trade conferences. Ask your friends in the industry what companies they recommend.

You can also look for books on Amazon about various topics. This is a great place to find subject matter experts and people with large audiences.

Get creative. Find more than you think you'll need. Find big names that scare you a little. It's in the fear and excitement that you will find the drive to move forward.

You should have no trouble finding more companies than you need.

The Reverse Interview

It's almost time to call the companies, but first I need to teach you what to say.

You need something easy that will catch their attention.

What would give you an "in"?

What would be hard to say "no" to?

I've come up with the perfect phrase to get the ball rolling.

Ready?

Here are the "9 Magic Words", complete with explanation, that will open virtually any door at any company.

Ready?

First three words:

I Would Love

"Love" is a very strong and definite word. It does not leave any room for doubt. It's a commitment. You're not saying, "I would like," or, "It would be nice," or any other wishy-washy, "I'm not so sure" phrase. You are claiming your ground.

Next three words:

To Interview You

Any idea what the key word here is? Without a doubt it's the word "You". You are stating that it's all about them. You are elevating their status immediately. You are letting them know that they are someone to be heard and understood.

Last three words:

For My Book

You are asking permission to record their experiences, knowledge and passion in a permanent medium ... a book. Books have stood the test of time over hundreds of years as a way to be seen as an authority. The word "my" lets them know that they don't even have to do the work; you will do it for them.

So the first thing you will say when you call the companies and reach out to your industry experts is:

"I would love to interview you for my book."

Now you have a conversation starter that sounds much better than a presentation about how great you are and how much you have done and how you could be such a benefit to their organization if only they would give you a chance to prove yourself, blah-blah-blah.

Talking about yourself is what everyone else does.

Asking about them is what virtually no one else does.

> *Extremely Important Side Note:*
>
> This is not a trick. This is not a game. This is a sincere outreach to key people that you would like to know, to learn from AND to teach other people about in the form of a book.
>
> Therefore, it is absolutely imperative that you remember this and adhere to this core objective

with every word you say and every thought you think. You are truly and completely interested in hearing and sharing what they have to say.

Do NOT think that once the door is open you can or should start hinting around at a job opening or you will destroy everything you've done so far.

Don't go there. Your time will come!

You have set yourself up as someone who cares, who is interested. Not only do you want to become better at what you do, you are willing to put in the extra effort. You're not after instant gratification.

I think you get it now.

After you say the "9 Magic Words", those industry leaders will want to know more about your book and why you're writing it.

This is where you not only tell them the title, but you explain why it matters to you and you offer to show them the 3D model of your book. You can also go into more detail about what you would like to hear about and what you want to convey to the readers. You should explain to each contact why you think he or she is a key component to the project (because you've also done your homework about the company, right?)

SUMMARY NOTES:

1. It's not who you know but who knows you that's most important.
2. Use your answers in the previous chapter to help come up with your title and subtitle.
3. Search online for inspiration for your title too.
4. Find something that gets you excited.
5. Create a virtual 3D image of your book.
6. Find your experts to interview.
7. Get some big names on your list even if you don't expect to work for them.
8. Learn the "9 Magic Words" to get interviews.
9. Explain your reason "why".
10. Remain in integrity, and focus on writing a great book.

COLLECT
To be interesting, be interested

"No one cares how much you know, until they know how much you care."

Theodore Roosevelt
Twenty-sixth United States President

This quote by Teddy Roosevelt is so true and perfect for what this book is all about. First, show others how much you care, and then they will care about how much you know, where you've been and what your goals and ambitions are.

What is a great way to show someone that you care?

Ask a good question.

And here is the hard part for most people.

Sit back and listen.

I mean *really* listen to what they have to say. Active listening means not only paying attention, but also exhibiting body language that shows you are listening. That means eye contact, head nodding, complete focus and occasionally paraphrasing what they said to make sure you got it right, and then validating that they have a good point or story.

The Reverse Interview

After you've done all those things, then you can ask your next question.

Sounds like a lot to remember, doesn't it?

It is all very natural if you care about the interviewee, the subject matter and the responses. Everything I listed is what you would do naturally about anything you're interested in. When you want to know about a subject and you're fully engaged, here is what you are NOT doing:

- Looking at your watch
- Checking your phone for messages
- Peeking out the window
- Thinking about what's for dinner
- Preparing your next question

Being fully present and being an active listener tells your expert interviewee that you care. He will want to give you more. She will dig deeper and give the true gems that will make your book valuable to your readers.

Here is an enormous side benefit.

As your subjects tell you their stories of struggles and triumph, they will feel the emotions that they had as they went through in their journeys. They will become emotional … maybe outwardly emotional, but certainly inwardly emotional.

Just like when you remember your first love and the music and movies associated with him/her, you will become associated with the feelings that you are bringing up in your experts.

It will be as though you were there when they founded the company, when they made their first sale or when their product or service helped to save a life. As they open up to you and tell you their story, you become a part of that story too.

There will be a bonding and a trust that will form if you do your part properly ... sit quietly and listen actively.

Side Note:

This is an advanced tip that very few people know about or fully understand. It is the secret to "accelerated relationship building."

Think about someone you know very well. It could be your spouse, or a friend or a relative or even a co-worker. Now think about how many settings you've seen that person in.

If you've only seen a co-worker in the work environment, you may think you know that person well. You really don't. You only know that person well as he or she displays himself or herself at work. To know anyone much better is to also go to lunch together, to go bowling, fishing, walking, to karaoke ... anything and everything.

That is why many of the best job interviewers, usually the people interviewing for key positions in their companies, will ask for multiple interviews in multiple settings. They may ask the applicant to dinner or to play golf. It gives them a chance to get to know the candidate better and accelerates their comfort level.

You can do the same thing with your expert. Even moving from their office to a conference room, talking outside to "get some fresh air" or going to lunch will increase their comfort level with and affinity for you.

Your primary role most of the time during the interview is to be an active listener, but you still must be aware and guide the process. You must have a flow of how you want the interview to go and have a list of open-ended questions to direct the interview through a procedure that creates their chapter in your book.

Interview Questions

There are three types of questions that you need to ask during the course of the interview:

1. Introduction and opening questions
2. Main body questions
3. Conclusion and call-to-action questions

Each serves its own purpose for the interview and together makes for a complete, well-rounded chapter for your book.

Here are the explanations and some examples of each type of question:

1. Introduction and opening questions

The first type of question (there should be just one or two) should set the stage for who they are, what they have accomplished, and why I (as the reader) would want to listen to them. It also serves to break the ice with the interviewees and get them more comfortable with the interview process. These should be very easy questions that they've answered or at least thought about many times before.

Examples:

Would you please tell me a little bit about yourself and how you got started?

When did you first decide that this industry was right for you?

2. Main body questions

The main body questions are where you delve more deeply into the main topic of your book. This is where you focus most of your time and attention. You want to make sure that you give your readers some really good, actionable information, and get your expert to dig deeply into his story and about why he does what he does. You need to dig out what really matters, and get him to tell you how he has been able to make an impact in his industry or community.

Examples:

What advice would you give to someone who's new to _____?

What is the biggest mistake you've made getting started in _____?

What would you say is the most important thing you've learned from your experience?

3. Conclusion and call to action questions

The last question or two will wrap things up. Give your expert a chance to fill in any gaps in the interview, and to add anything that she feels needs to be included. She should also have the chance to give her contact or product/service information so that the readers can find out more. After all, your experts are involved in business and you are helping them to get their message out.

Examples:

Is there anything else you'd like to cover that we missed so far?

Where can our readers find out more about you and/or your company?

The steps of the interview so far are pretty simple: come up with some good questions and be a good and active listener, but there is more to the process in order for the interview to not only go smoothly, but to have it in a format that can easily be put into a book.

Let's back up a bit, and set the stage more thoroughly to make the best of the whole process shall we?

Do you consider yourself to be an introvert or an extrovert?

Introverts- This may take you out of your comfort zone a little bit more than it does for the extroverts, but that's okay. This system was primarily developed for people like you.

While you may or may not feel comfortable conducting these interviews, understand that you probably have a key trait that extroverts often do not: you are a good listener by nature. You are good at taking in information without interrupting and needing to fill space with your own thoughts. This is absolutely a key ingredient to conducting a great interview.

As for being out of your element a bit ... all you need to do is remember that the interview is not about you, it is about your expert. You are not the one being grilled in a "normal" interview and being put on the spot to come up with the right answers and being judged for everything you say and do.

You are the one with the power, because the one who asks the questions is the one in charge.

All you need to do is remember this is all about the expert and is for the benefit of you and your readers. Let your natural instincts take over during the interview and listen intently. Trust your instincts to ask appropriate follow-up questions as needed and you will do great.

Extroverts- This may sound exciting for you to just jump in and get rolling! You are in your element. That is perfect. Getting started is the hardest part of any project and you will clear that hurdle with room to spare. You are comfortable talking to people (and in this case, interviewing people) and actually look forward to it.

You likely will connect with the experts with ease, as you are comfortable with the project, meeting lots of people and sharing your enthusiasm. Use all of these traits to your maximum benefit.

Here are my words of caution based on my experience with this process. You may have more trouble reigning yourself in during the interview and letting the focus be on your expert interviewee. You need to be an active listener and have your experts' voices be the focus of the conversations.

The main thing to remember for both introverts and extroverts is that the focus is on the expert interviewee. The spotlight and pressure are not on you. You just need to guide the conversation with your prepared questions and stay present with your active listening skills.

Both introverts and extroverts need to make sure your guests are comfortable with the interview. The best way to do this is by supplying them with the list of "suggested" questions beforehand. Make sure that they are happy with them and let them know that they can be modified as needed.

They may have a special story they'd like to tell, so you should have a question that helps lead into that tale. They may have some special way they'd like to close the interview, so you can accommodate that too.

When your guests know you are concerned about putting them in the best light possible and that you have no intention of any surprise questions, they will feel relaxed and ready to go.

Record the Interview

You will need to record the interview so that it can be transcribed later. There are many ways to do this. You could take a laptop with either a built-in microphone (not ideal) or a plug-in, external microphone for greatly improved clarity.

You could also use your smart phone if you have one, but don't expect great audio quality without adding an external microphone.

A better and definitely more professional looking setup would include a stand-alone, battery operated portable recorder. These are not very expensive and allow for easier, quicker recording. They usually have removable memory. Get a large internal memory chip to ensure all the recording time you could ever need.

Here are two examples of portable recorders by Tascam and Zoom. There are many more makes and models similar to these.

Portable Recorder Examples

Practice with a volunteer before using the recorder in a real-life situation. You need to be very familiar with not only how the recorder works, but where it should be placed during the interview. It is most important to clearly capture the words of your guest because you already know the questions you will be asking, and those can easily be recreated.

It might be helpful to have a small, flexible tripod to place the microphone on so that you have more options to get the setup right.

Flexible Tripod Example

Collect

The big scary part of authoring a book in the "normal" way is the weeks, months and sometimes years it takes slaving away and banging on a keyboard … that is, assuming you don't have writers block and just sit staring at the keypad instead.

Here's how *you* will get your book done.

Transcribe the audio!

While fiction authors are spending months and years and countless hours developing characters and story lines, you are handed your lead characters and all the interesting anecdotes a good writer could ever want.

Real people with real stories never go out of style. When they also serve the purpose of making connections and helping you, your readers and your experts, it's all a very nice bundle.

I told you earlier that labor is cheap, but creativity is expensive. Transcribing the audios is just labor… and it's very simple labor too, so it's cheap.

To transcribe the audio, you don't even have to do all the typing yourself. You can go to a site like Elance.com, or oDesk.com or even Fiverr.com to find good, qualified transcribers at very reasonable prices. Maybe you have a spouse or a child or a neighbor who would be willing to do it for you. If you want to save the money and you have the time, then you can always do it yourself.

I would suggest you transcribe each interview as you get it. Otherwise, the work will pile up and look too daunting. Plus you can experiment with different transcription methods. Maybe you want to do a few yourself or test a few people from the recommended sites until you find someone you enjoy working with.

Proofing and Editing

This is another area where it would be easy to spend way too much time, effort and money. Before hiring an editor, take a first pass and clean up as much as you can on your own. Word processing software such as Microsoft Word™ do a great job of pointing out spelling and grammatical errors, but don't take it as the gospel. Don't be afraid to ignore many of the changes it suggests.

Your style and the style of your experts will likely be more conversational (after all, it's a conversation that you're recording) and that's fine. Word™ may suggest many more changes than someone trying to produce a high-browed literary work of art.

Your book is about getting great information out to help people, not to impress them with your prose.

Once you've given your manuscript the once-over, send it to some friends or colleagues. Trust me, if there is anything wrong, they will find it and point it out to you. People seem to love finding errors in other people's work (You may have found a couple in this book ... hopefully not, but there always seems to be a few that sneak by).

If you really want to take it another step, go to one of the sites I mentioned before (oDesk.com, Elance.com) and pay a few bucks for a pro to go through your book ... just don't get so carried away that it doesn't get finished.

Give yourself a huge pat on the back!

You have done the hard parts: Connecting with the right people, recording their words of experience and wisdom and transcribing the words onto your computer.

Well done.

The next step is getting it out in a form where anyone and everyone can have access to it.

It's called publishing a book!

More specifically, publishing a book on Amazon.com.

It's easier, quicker and cheaper than you could possibly imagine.

SUMMARY NOTES:

1. Learn how to ask a good question and then actively listen.
2. Get your interviewee into an emotional state.
3. "Accelerated relationship building:" talk with your guest in multiple locations/settings if possible.
4. Use three types of questions for your interview flow: opening, body and conclusion.
5. The focus of the interview is always on the guest.
6. Record the interview with a portable recorder.
7. Transcribe the audio after each interview.
8. You now have all the text for your book.

CONVEY
Because it's NOT who you know that matters

> *"We know what we are, but know not what we may be."*
>
> **William Shakespeare**
> English poet, playwright and actor

This is the third of the three major steps in the process: Convey.

You've already connected with your desire and the people who have shown success in that area.

You've collected information from outstanding people that will skyrocket your network, connections and credibility in your chosen field.

Now you need to get the word out. You need to show the world how you are different from everyone else. You need proof that you can deliver and that you are a leader too.

Side note:

> A book came out in 2012 that is very useful to understand how it applies to the job market. The book is called "Pendulum" by Roy H. Williams

and Michael R. Drew.

PENDULUM
ROY H. WILLIAMS & MICHAEL R. DREW

"Startling insights and perspectives for anyone who wants to be successful now or in the future."
— Tony Hsieh, New York Times bestselling author of Delivering Happiness and CEO of Zappos.com

HOW PAST GENERATIONS SHAPE OUR PRESENT AND PREDICT OUR FUTURE

The authors studied human behavior and found that there is a cyclical swing that happens every eighty years. We move from a "We" generation to a "Me" generation and back again every eight decades.

During a "Me" generation, it's all about the individual. Back in the 1980s, we were in the midst of a "Me" generation and it was about proving to your potential boss what a super-hero you were. It was about degrees and accomplishments and single-handedly conquering all challenges.

But things have changed.

We are now in the upswing of a "We" generation. While it's still good to have degrees and accomplishments, now it's more about who you're connected to and how you can get a job done. In this internet-connected world, it's more about *finding* the answers rather than *being* the answer.

Your network is more important than you are. It's about collective solutions, not being superhuman.

Here is something that has gone unchanged for centuries, ever since there was a thing call a book ... those who write them are taken seriously. They are put into a special, elevated club above the less dedicated people.

It's a bit like graduating from college. Everyone knows it takes time, effort and commitment.

A book is a bit different than graduating from higher education though. Schools always have task masters (usually called teachers, instructors, or professors, or sometimes "SOBs") who force you to keep going. Plus, there is an implicit reward that awaits those who complete the journey: diploma, recognition, a job, etc.

Authors must have an inner force to drive them forward ... a mission ... a guiding light ... a principle that keeps them moving until their task is complete.

Companies often look for college graduates because they want a candidate who not only has knowledge, but enough drive and "grit" to see a task through to the end.

Watch a video to really understand about "grit" here:

ReverseInterview.com/bonus

Authors have grit too. It tells everyone that you are a person who can stick to a task, without supervision, until it is done.

This chapter is about how you can convey to the world that you are a leader and that you have grit and determination. It is also about proof of your connections, credibility and authority.

Publish Your Book

Perhaps the most important step is to publish your book. Basically, that means uploading two files to one website. That's it, and you're done.

Back in the "old days," you heard horror stories about going to dozens if not hundreds of publishers with your book in hopes of finding a sympathetic editor who believed in your vision. If you managed to find someone willing to publish your work, it would then take months and years of back and forth with contracts and edits and more.

That is no longer the case with self-published, print-on-demand companies. Now, there is:

No searching

No begging

No pleading

No rejection

No cost

No commitment

Upload your files and you, my friend, are a published author!

Very Important Side Note:

When you go through a traditional publisher, the publishing house actually owns your work, your book. If it does not sell as well as the publisher needs it to, the book can be taken out of print. That means you can no longer get copies of your own book.

Also, since the publisher owns the rights to your book, you cannot create derivative works related to the book without consent. You may want to create a workbook or give a seminar based on the book. You would most likely need to get permission to do these things.

When you self-publish your book, you have much more freedom, control and latitude to do the things you want to do.

Two Files

So what are the two files that you need to upload and how do you create them? The first one is the document you created in the last chapter. It's the transcript of the interviews with your guest experts. It's a text document.

Look at other books that you have lying around.

Look at how they are formatted. Look at the pages before and after the body of the book. Look at the table of contents. All you need to do is follow those templates instead of creating your own.

Or, I have a shortcut for you. Use my template, which you can download here:

ReverseInterview.com/bonus

It's my little gift to you for reading this far. Commitment has its rewards. This will get you going, but you can still customize it to match whatever style you like.

Cut and paste your text, chapter by chapter, into the template. Save the template with the name of your book and you now have the first of the two documents that you need to upload.

The second document?

Well, that would be the graphic file of the cover of your book. The file is the complete front cover, around the spine of the book and the back cover. It's one continuous file that wraps around three sides of the book.

In order to make sure that the file is the right size, just go to Createspace.com (the publisher we are going to use) and find your book size from its standard sizes (I suggest five inches by eight inches, since that matches the template size you just downloaded for the text on the inside) and enter the number of pages in your book.

The more pages you have, the thicker the book will

be and the wider the graphic file will need to be in order to wrap around the book properly. This is perhaps the trickiest part to get right, so that's not too bad. It beats setting type for weeks on end, doesn't it? Johannes Gutenberg, eat your heart out.

Take the book cover design that you created in the "Connect" chapter and have it fully designed to the proper size for print. Just go back to the designer you used before to get the quick version and flesh out the full cover, including the back side.

Again, find a book that you have and like the looks of, and use that as a template.

Createspace provides templates so that you know exactly where the "safe edges" are to print as well as where things like the bar code go. Go to my bonus section on the website to find a cover design with the Createspace template on it so you can see what I'm talking about.

The example is for a 5" x 8" book. You may need to download a different template from Createspace due the number of pages that your book has, but it's a great starting point to understand the process.

If you have some decent graphics skills with Adobe Photoshop or most any other image editing software, and an example book cover as a guide, you can knock out a great cover by yourself in a couple of hours. If not, just give all of this information to your designer.

Createspace will provide you with an ISBN number free of charge to put in your book. That's what makes your book a "real" book, and it gets you listed and found by anyone looking for your book.

Important Side Note:

It may be worth of a little extra money for you to buy your own ISBN number separately from Createspace. If you ever want to move your book to another publisher, you really can't do that if Createspace provided the ISBN ... they control it, not you.

Here is more information about Createspace and how to use the service. Owned by Amazon, it integrates very easily into their platforms, and your book can be listed on Amazon like every other book. There is even a special store that they provide where anyone can buy your books as well.

As the author, you can buy books at a very discounted rate. It doesn't matter if you buy one book, one hundred books or one thousand books ... you get the same low price. It's really amazing!

You can order your books now and get them in just a few days. But what should you do with them? I have some suggestions for you!

Social Proof

When we are uncertain, we often look to see what others are doing or what others think to help us form an opinion or choose which action to take. Social proof, in this context, is about showing the world that you are an author and that what you do matters. It's about being recognized for the work you've accomplished and the connections you've made. It's about being relevant in your industry. Having this kind of "social proof" gives people a favorable impression of you even before they meet you.

Most people do things in hopes of "being found" or "discovered." There are dozens of courses about LinkedIn and how to build a great presence there so that perspective employers will find you. You definitely should have a great LinkedIn profile. However, I wouldn't count on LinkedIn to be your best chance of landing a great job. Sitting back and waiting for someone to find you is not the best option.

I believe it's better to create your own future.

Therefore, the social media strategies I'm about to share with you are more about "proof" than "discovery." That means that once someone is interested in you (and they will be) they can very easily find more information about you, what you do, who you know and what you offer.

But guess what.

If you believe in all the good things that come from the "discovery" side, you'll have all of those benefits by following what I'm about to show you ... but it'll work ten times better for you as an author with abundant social proof avenues.

How many social media sites are out there now? There are hundreds, but there are a few that head the list. Among them are Facebook, LinkedIn, Twitter, Pinterest, Tumblr, Instagram and Google +.

Photos

Here's the first step that I recommend once your book is published and you have some copies in hand: Go back to one of your guest experts and give him a copy. Have your picture taken as you hand him your book.

There you are in a photo, handing your book to a well-known and respected person in your industry. It's priceless. You automatically have standing in that industry and specifically with that person.

Ask for a quote about how it was to work with you and what he thinks of your capabilities and your potential. Now you have a testimonial that you can put in print. In the job seekers' world, that testimonial is known as a reference.

What is the next step? Rinse and repeat. Go to every one of your guest experts and have that photo taken and get that testimonial. They will enjoy doing it for you and you will reap the benefits for decades!

Post your pictures in your LinkedIn and Facebook accounts. There will be even more strategies to use them later in the book!

Books in Batches

Want to know what else you should do while you're with each one of the experts?

Ask them how many copies of the book they would like to have to pass out to colleagues, friends and family.

You want your book in as many hands as possible and who beside yourself would be proud to show off this book? That's right; the people who helped you write it.

If you offer your book for sale on Amazon for

$19.95, it may actually only cost you about $3 or $4 per book to order copies directly from Createspace. You can choose to sell books to your experts for whatever price you choose. I would suggest you at least cover your costs, but you can add a couple of bucks to make a profit at the same time too. Why not? They don't know your cost and $6 for a $19.95 book is a great bargain.

Website

Buy the domain name that matches your book title. If that domain is not available, then buy the book title plus the word "book." Buy the ".com" domain for best results. Examples: YourBookTitle.com and YourBookTitleBook.com

Hollywood producers do the same thing with movies. You'll frequently see the title of a movie with the word "movie" at the end of the domain name because there are so many domain names already taken.

If you are good at building websites, then you are off to the races. I install WordPress on my domains and go from there. If you're not technically inclined, then find a web designer from a site like Elance.com and spend a few bucks to put up a nice, professional looking site. You could also use a free service like Wordpress.com, Weebly.com or Wix.com to build your site yourself very easily.

If you choose to hire out the work, find several book sites that you would like to model and send them to your web person to do it for you.

The main point is to have a professional looking site that you can point people to when they have an interest in you or that they will find when they search for you or your book. It's all about building credibility.

Press Releases

Now that you have your book, and even during the interviewing process, you can use the power of press releases to get the word out about what you are doing.

One of the biggest reasons for press releases is the weight they carry in the SEO (Search Engine Optimization) world. That means when people search for you they find you near the top of the list in the search results.

Why does this matter?

Again, it's about credibility. When people search for you and you appear over and over in the search results, you naturally carry more clout.

I like to go to Fiverr.com and search for "press release." There are numerous providers who will write and/or submit your press release for you at a very reasonable price.

Some of the better press release sites charge a significant amount of money, upwards of $100. They also tend to get better results because the search engines pay a little more attention to them.

I suggest that you go with the low-cost Fiverr method to get your press release written, and then try Fiverr for the submission. If you're not happy with the results, and don't mind paying a larger fee, try one of the other press release firms.

Other Social Proof Methods

You are limited only by your time, money and creativity. I'll give you a few more ideas to spark your creative thoughts.

It is absolutely NOT necessary to do all of these … or any, for that matter. These are all just "extras" to get yourself out there where people will find you. The more you do the more you will be found and the better your chances will be of landing that ideal job.

Pick what looks interesting, easy and fun, then do it. Leave the others behind or pick them up later if you want more activity with your career search. It's completely up to you!

Book Launch Party: Invite your friends, readers, city mayor, local newspaper etc. to a big launch party. Set it up at a local hotel and have it catered. Hire a photographer to capture the whole affair. Get your picture taken with all of the attendees, especially the better-known people. Give away personally signed books.

Pictures are "proof" that you exist and that people care about you. Look for opportunities to get them. You'll find countless ways to use them. I'll show you a few creative ways to use them in a later chapter.

Blogging: I would suggest that you set up a blog section on your book website. You can take sections of your book and include them in your blog. Write about your thoughts and what your co-authors were saying in their interviews. Talk about yourself, what you do and your passions outside your profession.

Post regularly, whether that's once a day or once a week (though more is usually better, consistency is the key).

Blogging is not only another way for the search engines to find you, it's also a way for your readers (aka: potential employers) to get to know you and what you stand for. Resumes have a very low limit as to what people are willing to read because they're in the mode of weeding them out. A blog, on the other hand, will draw people in and get them interested in what you have to say.

Article writing: Want to make a big splash in a big way in a small amount of time? Of course you do! One of the best ways is to find a publication in your field and offer to write a guest article for it.

Look offline for physical publications that serve your audience. They need content and are happy to have good writers with industry experience provide it for them. Call to see what topics are coming up in future issues that you could help with.

Not a great writer? That's not a problem either. Go to a service like Elance.com and find someone to write the article for you. They will research similar articles and put together something for you that will be near perfect.

Want it to have a more personal touch? Take the article that you had written for you and re-write it in your own voice and add your own color to it. Writing from scratch can be a chore, but touching up something that's already written is a snap.

Don't limit yourself to just printed magazines, though!

Look online for e-zines and blogs in your industry. They have several very important characteristics for you. They are abundant. They usually have a lower threshold for having an article accepted. They can be much quicker to post your article, since an all-digital publication can be processed much more quickly. Plus, being online, it's searchable and easy to find and distribute.

Summary Notes:

1. Get the word out.
2. We are in a "We" Generation and connections often are more important than the individual.
3. Authors are seen as leaders, self-starters and are committed to seeing difficult projects through to completion.
4. Authors have grit.
5. Traditional publishing is difficult and takes a lot of time.
6. Self-publishing is quick, easy and inexpensive.
7. Self-publishing does not have the limitations of traditional publishing.
8. Use social proof with the books and your experts.
9. Have pictures taken with you, your book and your experts.
10. Sell quantities of books to your experts to have or give away.
11. Create a website about your book.
12. Distribute press releases.
13. Have a book launch party.
14. Blog about your book and experiences.
15. Write and publish articles.

The Reverse Interview

Section 3
SYSTEM APPLICATION

WEAPONS OF MASS INFLUENCE
Human nature doesn't change, but you can

> *"When you make your peace with authority, you become authority."*
>
> **Jim Morrison**
> American singer-songwriter and poet

Robert Cialdini wrote a book in 1984 that has become a bit of a standard amongst marketers and is still very popular today. It's called "Influence: The Psychology of Persuasion".

Marketing is one of the biggest expenses (other than salaries, goods and taxes) that many companies have. It is usually on the order of ten to twelve percent of gross profit of the organization. That means there is a lot of emphasis placed on getting it right.

There is a lot of money at stake here to be made or lost. There is no shortage of marketing books, courses and degrees to help companies outpace their competitors and take a bigger piece of the pie without losing their shirts.

If Cialdini's book rises to the top of the must-read list, then I pay attention.

Did I lose you?

Why am I talking about marketing?

Because while other job seekers are running around answering ads and mailing resumes like a desperate person lost in a sea of noise and confusion, you are going to use the tactics of billion dollar companies to outpace them all.

Make no mistake; you are marketing yourself when you are looking for a job. You can learn a few simple things that work, or you can waste your time and be ignored. It's your choice.

Fortunately for you, you've already done the work. This chapter is merely to explain what it is you've done and how it applies to Cialdini's ground breaking work in the psychology of persuasion.

According to Cialdini's research of hundreds of companies and their tactics, it all boils down to six "Weapons of Influence" as he called them:

1. Reciprocation
2. Commitment and Consistency
3. Social Proof
4. Liking
5. Authority
6. Scarcity

Weapons of Mass Influence

Using any of these weapons allows you to gain influence over another person. Companies use them in their marketing to persuade people to buy from them. Any one technique is sufficient to turn a casual passerby into a customer.

In your case, using any one of these methods will grab the attention of a potential employer to take a closer look at you. It will put the odds in your favor, not only to be noticed, but also to "influence" them to take the next step with you.

If you want more influence, use more of the six weapons that you have at your disposal. By following the steps outlined in this book, you brilliantly have used all six of the weapons.

You are a job-seeking ninja!

Let's take a look at each of the six weapons and how you have used them to your favor already.

Reciprocation

Reciprocation is a mutual exchange or a return of similar value. In our social culture, it also implies that if someone does something for you there is a feeling of responsibility to return the gesture.

Take a walk through the food court at your local mall. Chances are very good that there will be people standing in the aisle offering free tastes of the food their restaurants are serving.

At first glance, you may think it's just so you can have a sample to make an informed decision about whether you want to buy the full meal. However, that's only the beginning of the strategy and only a portion of why it works.

After taking the free sample, there's a little voice that kicks in that says, "Well, it tasted pretty good. It may not be exactly what I wanted today, but they were so nice to offer it to me maybe I'll go ahead and eat there."

Okay, maybe that's not exactly what goes on in your head, but something like it happens to enough people to make it worth the vendor's time, effort and money to keep giving away his food. People buy more meals after first being given a sample, and it's largely due to the principle of reciprocity: he did something for me now I should do something for him.

Start paying attention and you'll see examples everywhere. There is a whole industry that sells items for companies to give away to customers and prospects. They're usually custom printed just so you'll remember their names and where to go back and spend your money. Examples include coffee mugs, pens, fans, T-shirts, bags, USB drives, magnets and on and on. Giving these items away is more than just advertising, it's the reciprocity factor put into action.

How does this apply to the Reverse Interview?

You just gave your time and attention to an industry expert. You are spending even more time and effort publishing a book about her, her views, her successes and her story.

If someone writes about herself and her accomplishments, it's seen as bragging. What you say about yourself is discounted, but what others say about you is believed and trusted.

Therefore, you are providing a service for the expert that she cannot do for herself: third-party validation. What is that worth? It's worth more than money.

Reciprocity is an unwritten contract that must be balanced. You have tipped the scale in your direction; now there is tension and social pressure for your expert to return the scale to neutral.

Ever been given an unexpected present for Christmas?

It feels more than a little bit awkward … Makes you want to get back to even in a hurry, doesn't it? That's the same tension that you create for your expert, but without the awkwardness. He just feels compelled to do something for you in return.

What he does for you could be as big as offering you a job, or it could be something much simpler like giving you a testimonial (reference) or introducing you to another key contact. Either way you come out a winner.

Score #1 in your favor – great start!

Commitment and Consistency

This principle is not as well understood and harder to see examples of in the real world, but it is no less powerful.

I once taught a course and led live seminars for small businesses to teach them how to get video testimonials from satisfied clients. The most obvious advantage for doing this is the testimonial itself and the ability of the testimonial to influence additional prospects to trust them and buy their products and/or services.

But there is another potent psychological trigger taking hold in the background.

Once someone has taken a stance on something, it is very difficult to get them to change that position. They have just put down an anchor with the weight of their word on it.

Therefore, when John goes on record as saying "XYZ Company has a great product and a great team behind it," he will try very hard to make sure that he doesn't deviate from that stance later. He is now honor bound to make sure that he is right. He will defend his position against all naysayers.

This is "commitment and consistency." It is taking a stance (commitment) and then sticking with it (consistency).

Your expert has welcomed you and trusted you to tell her story (commitment). Now she is on your side and will stick with you, and therefore her decision when things come up about you in the future (consistency). She will want to be right about her trust in you.

She will recommend you. She will be a great referral when you need one. She is on your side.

Score #2 for you – keep going!

Social Proof

When people are faced with a decision and feel they

have insufficient information to make a good choice, they often defer to others whom they assume have more facts than they do. In other words, they look for social proof.

Let's see what this looks like in practice.

You are in an unfamiliar town. It's getting to be around lunchtime and you're getting hungry. As you drive down the road you see two very similar looking restaurants. They're both about the same size and age, and they serve the same cuisine. It's really a toss-up as to which place you should choose.

But then you see a striking difference!

One restaurant has two cars in front of it and the other has fifteen cars all around it. Surely these are local people and they know much more than you do. There is obviously a good reason so many cars are at one place and not the other. Naturally, you decide to get lunch at the more popular restaurant.

Bam! You've just been hit with social proof!

It's the same reason online companies such as Amazon.com put so much effort into getting reviews for every product on their site. We all put stock in other people's opinions … third-party proof about something we don't know enough about.

It should be no surprise at this point what you've done to create your own social proof. There were several specific examples in the prior chapter about how to add even more. But just to make sure you have this hammered down, let's recap.

1. You have a book with expert co-authors.
2. Your name is seen alongside experts.
3. You have pictures giving your book to known experts.
4. You have a website with your book and reviews.
5. Your book is for sale on Amazon.
6. Your name and book are found near the top of web searches.
7. You have a blog.
8. You have written articles for leading online and offline publishers.

All these are examples of social proof and making it easier for someone to choose you ahead of anyone else.

Score #3 in multiple major ways – let's keep the momentum going!

Liking

It should be no surprise that people you like have influence over you.

Here's a real world example that affects more than fifteen thousand doctors each year. You might be a bit shocked about this one.

Doctors are often the target of huge malpractice suits. Damages can be in the tens of thousands to millions of dollars range. According to a study I read by attorney Martin Pringle, the top reasons doctors are sued have nothing to do with incompetence. Rather, it's communication skills and bedside manner.

You read that right, it's more about whether patients

like, trust and believe in the doctor than about the details of what happened. People are reluctant to punish people they like. The flip side of the coin is: people want to reward the people that they do like.

What is there not to like about you from your experts' viewpoint? You've shared time together, you are helping to promote them, you are giving your expertise to write a book and publish it with their story in it. Let's face it, you've just made yourself very likeable.

Score #4 – They like you. What's next?

Authority

Authority figures have influence over you. Why else would your heart start to race when you see those flashing blue lights in your rear view mirror? That police officer is an authority with the power to take your money and/or your freedom.

What about all those letters after people's names on their business cards?

MD	PhD
BSEE	CPA
MBA	DDS
OB/GYN	DVMS

... And about a million more I could have listed.

Why do people put those letters on their cards after their signatures and post their degrees on their walls?

It shows authority. It shows that they have studied in

a particular area and have been recognized for their achievements.

If you have any extra letters you can put after your name, I suggest that you use them. It gives you a little bump (maybe a big bump) in credibility and authority.

Now you have something else to boost your authority!

What is the root word of "authority?" AUTHOR!

You authored a book, which automatically, by definition, makes you an authority on your subject. You are an authority in your chosen field.

Just like getting a degree is recognized as taking a lot of time, effort and study, writing a book also is seen as a rite of passage into a different league … and higher social stature. Throughout the last few centuries or more, authors have been held in high regard for their superior knowledge and perseverance.

Welcome to the big leagues!

Score #5 – Only one more to go. Can we make it a clean sweep?

Scarcity

Human beings are a very strange lot, aren't we? We can behave in some very peculiar, but predictable ways.

Halfway through your last Thanksgiving dinner, you just noticed there is only one roll left on the serving platter. Those tasty, homemade yeast rolls have been your favorite ever since you can remember … and

Weapons of Mass Influence

they're almost gone.

You've already eaten two, and you have one left on your plate. But now you're afraid you might not get another chance. What if you need just one more roll for dessert to put some butter and jelly on? What if someone else is eyeing that last roll, too?

At the risk of looking like a glutton, you put that last roll on your plate. Ahhh ... now you can continue with your meal without having to worry about losing that last mound of yeast, butter and wheat heaven.

This is what is known as the "fear of loss." Scarce items are naturally in more demand. It's a major motivating factor to get people to take action.

What does this look like in marketing? (Hint: you see it everywhere every day!)

"Limit five per customer"

> You only wanted one before, but now you think you should get all five so you don't miss out. You may even test their resolve and try buying ten!

"The Twinkie factory is closing"

> No more Twinkies! How Awful! You don't remember the last time you had a Twinkie. You don't think you even like them. You know it's not the healthiest choice ever, but if you don't buy another box right now, you may never get another chance!

"It's the last week to see this play before it's closed forever"

The show has been playing for the last seven years. You've never had more than a passing interest in seeing it before, but now it's your last chance. It's now or never. Not only that, but you're afraid other people are going to think the same thing. Those tickets are going to be hard to get. You'd better get one right now!

What the heck happened? It makes no sense! You only needed one, you don't like Twinkies, and you never wanted to see that play during the last seven years ... but you bought five (they wouldn't let you buy ten), you purchased a case of Twinkies, and you took your whole family to see the play.

It's scarcity. We want more of that which we can't have.

So how does this work for you in your job search?

There's only one you!

There is a limit of only one no matter how many employers want you. The time to hire you is now before someone else does. This window of opportunity may never open again.

What changed is that the whole world knows about you now. You're an expert in your industry, you do things for others first, they say good things about you, your accomplishments are seen everywhere, you're likable, you have a vast network of important people, and you've written a book ... and there's only one you.

Score #6 – A clean sweep. You've used every weapon in the arsenal of ways to gain influence over others.

You need to understand that human nature doesn't change. We all want the same things for the same reasons.

But *you* have changed.

You have become very desirable. Even though you may be the exact same person with the exact same experience, you now stand out above your peers.

You've used all six weapons of influence. Nicely done!

SUMMARY NOTES:

1. Robert Cialdini discovered six weapons of influence.
2. You have already used all six by following the steps in this book.
3. Reciprocation - provide value first, see what comes back.
4. Commitment and Consistency - Take a stance and stick with it.
5. Social Proof - a short cut to decision making.
6. Liking – it's just being likable.
7. Authority - Root word "Author".
8. Scarcity - There is only one you.

LEVERAGE
How to make (nearly) everything you do more effective

"The time is always right to do the right thing."

Dr. Martin Luther King Jr.
American pastor, activist and humanitarian

Make no mistake about this point: having a book of your own gives many opportunities for leverage!

> **Leverage**
> Lev•er•age ˈlev (ə) rij
> Definition: Use (something) to maximum advantage.

Throughout this book, we have talked about a unique way to be found for a job. We haven't talked much about what everyone else focuses on when trying to find a job.

Here is a list:

- Networking
- Business Cards
- Resume Writing
- Cover Letters

- Social Media (LinkedIn, Facebook)
- How You Dress
- Body Language
- How to Answer Interview Questions
- Follow Up After the Interview
- How to Use Job Boards
- How to use Headhunters
- And dozens more …

But you are no ordinary job seeker; you are an author. Does that mean you don't need to worry about all the things on this list?

Maybe, or maybe not.

I'm including this chapter as a way for you to cover all your bases. You may already have your dream job by now. You've interviewed and created relationships with a dozen or more key people in your industry. It's highly likely that you won't need this chapter at all, but …

I put this chapter here to make absolutely sure that you have the tools you need to find the job you want now, and that you know how to position yourself constantly for the next, bigger and better position.

Let's go through the list item by item. I'll show you how having a book will help you get maximum advantage out of each of these situations.

Networking

There are lots of ways to network. It could be a casual conversation while waiting in a doctor's office or it could be a formal function specifically for business people or even job networking.

The principles of effective networking are the same. You want to leave a lasting, positive impression on the people you meet. You never know who might be in a position to help you now or later. You never know what connections the person you are talking to at any given time has.

The mistake too many people make is trying to hog the conversation and fill it with self-aggrandizing hyperbole (read: BS about you) in an effort to impress them.

It doesn't usually work very well that way. People are most impressed with themselves and appreciate those who listen to them talk. So let them talk and then casually mention you have a book about _____ and you would like to give them a copy if they or someone they know could benefit from reading it.

Now you've not only left them with a positive first impression, but you've given them a lasting reminder of who you are and an obligation (remember reciprocation?) to read it or pass it on to someone specific who could use that information.

Go the extra step of signing it for them, and it's now in a different league. It's a treasured keepsake.

Business Cards

Almost everyone has a business card and most of the cards conform to the normal size and shape to look and store just like everyone else's card.

Boring ... and most business cards are filed as soon as the recipient gets home. Filed in the "circular" file, that is.

But what if you started using your book as your business card? It's obviously not the same size and shape as everyone else's. It is going to stick out, be noticed and share a different space in the owner's mind and pocket.

Unlike business cards, books rarely ever are thrown away. Just as in the networking situation, make sure you ask the recipient of your book to pass it on to someone who can use it once they have read it. They'll help you find the best owner for it; someone they know that's in your industry.

Your book will live on someone's bookshelf for years and be noticed by countless other people.

Resume Writing

Writing and updating your resume always seems to be the first thing on the to-do list when the need of a job change becomes apparent. It's the Number One tool in the toolbox for the task of telling people a little bit about you and that you're available.

Resume writing has become a huge industry full of books and services to help you get that "perfect" resume done. The promise is that you will have scores of people begging to hire you because of the beauty and grace and excellence of your resume.

Let me put it this way: if you are looking for a job by sending out resumes, you are already putting yourself in a losing position. Eighty percent of jobs are never listed and therefore are never open for resume submission.

If you still choose to go this route (and I doubt that

you will need to) you have a huge advantage over more than ninety-nine percent of those applying for that position.

Send your book along with your resume ... or even use the book *instead* of your resume. It WILL get noticed; it WON'T be tossed aside.

If you have someone interested in you because they found you through the social proof campaigns that you implemented ("Convey" chapter) then you already have a very hot lead. Send the book and follow up with a phone call. They'll want to hear more from you.

In almost every situation that requires a resume, send your book. It is your big differentiator.

Cover Letters

There is so much written about cover letters and much of it is contradictory. Some say that the cover letter is dead. Others say that it's much more important than your resume.

I say ... drum roll please ... send your book! A brief cover letter is great so that they understand more of who you are and why you'd be perfect for the job, but the book is going to speak louder than any cover letter or resume.

Social Media (LinkedIn, Facebook, etc.)

Social media is all the rage right now and rightly so. There is tons of information out there about so many potential candidates. Good information and bad ... I'll get back to that in a minute.

Many people are found through social media for open positions, particularly on LinkedIn. It is worthwhile to make sure you have profiles both on LinkedIn and on Facebook.

There are scores of people who make a very good living by advising job seekers about how to fill out their social media profiles. Here's an obvious hint: put your best stuff out there to be found. The more you have the better off you'll be.

Here is where you are waiting for me to say, "list your book," right? Well, I don't want to disappoint you. YES! List your book, but now you have a zillion other options to go along with it.

Put up pictures of your book.

List your book website.

Put up your pictures with big-hitters in your industry (you have these from a prior tip I gave you).

Include the articles that you've written.

Includes snippets from the book.

Use everything that you've done in the social proof section and add them into your profile wherever possible.

Potential employers are going to search to find out everything they can about you after they discover you and before they make you an offer. Make sure your social media slate is squeaky clean. What you thought was just for your friends to find may be in places you never expected.

Sometimes the best strategy to cover up a mistake you made somewhere is to overwhelm it with good press. The more good images and information you spread about yourself, the more likely it will outweigh anything and everyone else.

How You Dress

This is an interesting topic. I'm hoping it's fairly obvious that you should dress appropriately for the job you want … or dress a little better.

During a "normal" job interview, your interviewer is keenly interested in finding some way to reject you. Why? Because it makes his life easier. There is no risk in telling you "no."

If you look like a "yes" there is a lot more work to do.

Let your book do your talking before you ever walk into a "normal" interview. They will have the "yes" in their mind already and will be looking at you as a top candidate to begin with. The way you dress will be a much smaller factor.

Body Language

Yes, there are people who read into your body language. As much as 93% of communication is non-verbal. It's another way to discount you as early in the process as possible.

Read the "How to Dress" section above and it applies the same way here.

How to Answer Interview Questions

Many books have been written on this subject too.

Numerous places on the web will give you the most important and frequently asked questions. They'll also list the proper responses and the responses that will get you kicked out of the interview process.

There is a good chance you are here in an interview situation because you have made great impression on someone else higher up in the company with the Reverse Interview process. Now they have sent you through the "normal" route so that you can meet other people in the organization and so that he/she can get other opinions.

The knowledge you gained from industry experts during your interviews will give you a great edge here. You can not only give a great answer, but also cite the source where you learned it.

Follow Up After the Interview

Yes, you should always follow up after the interview. If it is a company that you already interviewed for your book, you've got a huge "in."

If it is another company, make sure you thank them and remind them of the connections you have. Instead of just going after the job, ask if you could connect them with any of your other contacts. Mention how you have some ideas that could help them with some open projects they have going on.

Be of service first. Make them want to talk to you again. You are a key person in this industry now and you can do great things for them. Demonstrate that you are different. You care. You want to help even if they don't hire you.

How to Use Job Boards

Alas, the job boards. It's the easiest way for job seekers to fool themselves into believing that they are out there looking for a job.

Each job listing on a job board gets an average of three hundred to four hundred applicants per day. First understand this: employers tend to use job boards as a last resort because no one wants to go through three thousand resumes every two weeks. Second, you don't want to be in a batch of three thousand resumes.

Yes, people get hired that way every day. Yes, people win the lottery every day too. It's not to say you shouldn't play the game, but if you do, at least realize the low probability of a positive outcome and whenever possible, stack the deck in your favor ...

Send a book

Or a link to your book

Or a link to your website

Or a link to your LinkedIn Profile

Or your press releases

Do anything and everything that shows you are not like the other three thousand people who posted for that job.

If you can find out who is offering the position, bypass the job board altogether. Go interview someone at that company for your next book ... and leave a copy of your current book.

How to Use Headhunters

Headhunters work for the hiring companies. They are there to fill an open spot. The good news is that, generally, they already have a good relationship with the company and their opinion counts much more than a random resume that is sent in.

They are also the ones that are much more likely to be searching in social media to find you. Everything that you've done there will be a great asset to you. It will help you get found and it will help impress them to send you through.

You should also proactively find the headhunters who specialize in your industry. Call them and send them a book. Let them know what you're looking for. They most likely will never go looking for a position you can fill, but they will remember you first when a slot opens up that's made just for you.

The list that looked so daunting at the beginning of this chapter now looks easy and fun. You've turned the process around so that it works WITH you, not AGAINST you.

Well played!

SUMMARY NOTES:

1. Get leverage on all the "normal" job seeking activities.
2. Use your book as a networking tool.
3. Your book becomes your business card.
4. Include your book with every resume, or instead of your resume.
5. Cover letters? They are just a personalized prelude for your book.
6. Social Media is great; enhance your posts with the pictures you've taken of yourself with the gurus of your industry.
7. How to dress ... that's for the other people to worry about now.
8. Body language ... just another disqualifier that barely pertains to you now.
9. Interview Questions – You can cite experts that you've spent time with.
10. Follow up after the interview - offer connections, be of service.
11. Job Boards - Use a battery of tools to stand above the hundreds of others posting.
12. Headhunters - Leave them a copy of your book to remember you when an opening hits their desks.

THE BIG GOAL
No one can ever move your career (cheese) again

"If you work hard at your job you'll make a living. If you work hard on yourself, you'll make a fortune."

Jim Rohn
Entrepreneur, author and motivational speaker

It's so easy to get caught up in your day-to-day activities and forget to look in front of you to see where you're heading and what your future may hold … or to "read the tea leaves," as they say.

Students in college often think that the world is waiting breathlessly for them to graduate and sweep them away to employment bliss and their lives will be filled with joy and money forever.

Employees working for a big, stable company believe that as long as they do a great job and get good reviews that their positions will last forever.

In many (most) cases, neither is true.

It is always prudent to be the captain of your own ship, even if you draw your paycheck from someone else. You should know what you want to do, grow in whatever position you have and constantly be on the

The Reverse Interview

lookout for changes on the horizon ... changes of your choice and changes that will happen without your consent.

This is the perfect time to tell you about "Who Moved My Cheese." You may have read this book already. If not, or if you would like a refresher, here is a summary

(Reprinted from Wikipedia)

> Allegorically, *"Who Moved My Cheese?"* features four characters: two mice, "Sniff" and "Scurry," and two little people (miniature humans in essence), "Hem" and "Haw." They live in a maze (a representation of one's environment) and look for cheese (a representative of happiness and success).
>
> Initially without cheese, each group, the mice and humans, paired off and traveled the lengthy corridors searching for cheese. One day both groups happen upon a cheese-filled corridor at "Cheese Station C." Content with their find, the humans establish routines around their daily intake of cheese, slowly becoming arrogant in the process.
>
> One day Sniff and Scurry arrive at Cheese Station C to find no cheese left, but they are not surprised. Noticing the cheese supply dwindling, they have mentally prepared beforehand for the arduous but inevitable task of finding more cheese. Leaving Cheese Station C behind, they begin their hunt for new cheese together.
>
> Later that day, Hem and Haw arrive at Cheese Station C

The Big Goal

only to find the same thing, no cheese. Angered and annoyed, Hem demands, "Who moved my cheese?" The humans have counted on the cheese supply to be constant, and so are unprepared for this eventuality.

After deciding that the cheese is indeed gone they get angry at the unfairness of the situation and both go home starved. Returning the next day, Hem and Haw find the same cheeseless place. Starting to realize the situation at hand, Haw thinks of a search for new cheese. But Hem is dead set in his victimized mindset and dismisses the proposal.

Meanwhile, Sniff and Scurry have found "Cheese Station N," new cheese. Back at Cheese Station C, Hem and Haw are affected by their lack of cheese and blame each other for their problem. Hoping to change, Haw again proposes a search for new cheese. However, Hem is comforted by his old routine and is frightened about the unknown.

He knocks the idea again. After a while of being in denial, the humans remain without cheese. One day, having discovered his debilitating fears, Haw begins to chuckle at the situation and stops taking himself so seriously.

Realizing he should simply move on, Haw enters the maze, but not before chiseling "If You Do Not Change, You Can Become Extinct" on the wall of Cheese Station C for his friend to ponder.

Still fearful of his trek, Haw jots "What Would You Do If You Weren't Afraid?" on the wall and, after thinking about that, he begins his venture. Still plagued with worry (perhaps he has waited too long to begin his search ...), Haw finds some bits of cheese that nourish him and he is able to continue his search.

Haw realizes that the cheese has not suddenly vanished, but has dwindled from continual eating. After a stop at an empty cheese station, Haw begins worrying about the unknown again. Brushing aside his fears, Haw's new mindset allows him to again enjoy life.

He has even begun to smile again! He is realizing that "When you move beyond your fear, you feel free." After another empty cheese station, Haw decides to go back for Hem with the few bits of new cheese he has managed to find.

Uncompromising, Hem refuses the new cheese, to his friend's disappointment. With knowledge learned along the way, Haw heads back into the maze. Getting deeper into the maze, inspired by bits of new cheese here and there, Haw leaves a trail of writings on the wall. These clarify his own thinking and give him hope that his friend will find aid in them during his search for new cheese.

Still traveling, Haw one day comes across Cheese Station N, abundant with cheese, including some varieties that are strange to him, and he realizes he has found what he is looking for. After eating, Haw reflects on his experience. He ponders a return to see his old friend. But Haw decides to let Hem find his own way. Finding the largest wall in Cheese Station N, he writes:

The Big Goal

> **Change Happens**
> *They Keep Moving the Cheese*
>
> **Anticipate Change**
> *Get Ready For the Cheese to Move*
>
> **Monitor Change**
> *Smell the Cheese Often So You Know When It Is Getting Old*
>
> **Adapt To Change Quickly**
> *The Quicker You Let Go Of Old Cheese, The Sooner You Can Enjoy New Cheese*
>
> **Change**
> *Move with the Cheese*
>
> **Enjoy Change!**
> *Savor The Adventure And Enjoy The Taste Of New Cheese!*
>
> **Be Ready To Change Quickly and Enjoy It Again**
> *They Keep Moving The Cheese.*
>
> Cautious from past experience, Haw now inspects Cheese Station N daily and explores different parts of the maze regularly to prevent any complacency from setting in. After hearing movement in the maze one day, Haw realizes someone is approaching the station. Unsure, Haw hopes that it is his friend Hem who has found the way.

Your cheese is a moving target. It's either going to move because you decide to go after something bigger and better, or someone is going to move it for you because of economic conditions, management change or any number of other possible reasons.

I left my first job after being there for about five years. I made myself a promise that I would evaluate myself and my position at the five-year mark to see if I should change direction regardless of whether I was happy there.

Once I took a look at what I was learning, the value of the knowledge to my current company and how transferable the knowledge was if the company folded (or if I was let go, etc.), I became very concerned.

My analysis showed that the things I was learning were making me more and more valuable to that company, but less valuable to other companies.

I felt I was painting myself into a corner, but I had the foresight and discipline to look around and see what was happening … and I didn't like it.

I was concerned.

It was time to look for new cheese.

For me, this is a critical realization in the story by Haw:

"When you move beyond your fear, you feel free."

You absolutely must be willing to look around to find out where you are and where you'd like to be. Once you get this figured out, you must be willing to take action.

The whole process that I've outlined in this book will probably move you out of your comfort zone, and

The Big Goal

that's a good thing.

You see, everything you have now is there because it's in your comfort zone. Everything you want is outside of your comfort zone.

Fear is crossing what Bob Proctor (from the movie *"The Secret"*) calls the "terror barrier." It's moving from your comfort zone out into the rest of the world … and it can be quite uncomfortable, but at the same time, that's where your freedom lies.

Freedom is the power of choice and the lack of limitations.

Freedom is choosing your own path and following it wherever it leads.

There is no faster way to grow and learn than by leveraging what others have done. Don't just follow in their footsteps, but allow your predecessors to lift you up and accelerate your pace toward your goals. They won't do this for just anyone, but they will gladly help someone willing to help themselves.

After all of the books I've read, the research I've done and the people I've talked to, I learned something. There is no better or faster way to put yourself into a respected position of authority than to associate with the people you'd like to emulate.

Use what you've learned in this book to help yourself to get your first job out of college regardless of your GPA or current connections.

Use the tactics here to investigate possibilities that you are considering moving into. What better way to see what a job really is all about than to interview the people who are doing and managing that job.

It's the perfect way to change careers. Use what you've learned to test a new vocation. If you like it, then continue to build connections and establish yourself in a brand new area.

Boost the career you're in right now. If you like what you're doing, why not find others who can accelerate your career by leveraging what they know. This initiative will look great to your manager and to the CEO.

Four-step process

1. Pick your goals.
2. Find the people who are already there.
3. Find out what they do.
4. Do those things.

Summary Notes:

1. Always look forward to see where your career is heading.
2. Make sure you are steering a course toward your goals.
3. "Who Moved My Cheese" is a great story about what can happen if you get complacent.
4. Your cheese (happiness and success) is always going to be moving.
5. Be willing to constantly move beyond your fear.
6. Freedom is the power of choice and the lack of limitations.
7. Leverage what others have done to accelerate your growth.

Section 4
WRAP IT UP

The Reverse Interview

BONUS CHAPTER
Simplify and simply get it done!

"We should be taught not to wait for inspiration to start a thing. Action always generates the inspiration."

Frank Tibolt
Writer, motivator and success trainer

Are you intimidated or overwhelmed by the thought of writing a book? Would you like to get similar results and get to interview top talent in your industry without the concern or pressure of turning your discussions into a book?

I have some alternate choices for you. They will be much easier to start and to complete, but they do have some limitations and they don't set you up as well for the long term credibility and trust that authoring a book would give you.

Any of these options is a much better course than doing nothing and may just give you the boost you need.

I suggest that if the book idea is keeping you from getting started, then choose one of these easier strategies. Get started and see if you then feel more comfortable moving toward the book later.

Do you remember the "9 Magic Words" from the "Connect" chapter? If not, here's a refresher:

> First three words:
>
> **I Would Love**
>
> "Love" is a very strong and definite word. It does not leave any room for doubt. It's a commitment. You're not saying, "I would like," or "It would be nice," or any other wishy-washy "I'm not so sure" phrase. You are claiming your ground.
>
> Next three words:
>
> **To Interview You**
>
> Any idea what the key word here is? Without a doubt it's the word "You". You are stating that it's all about them. You are elevating their status immediately. You are letting them know that they are someone to be heard and understood.
>
> Last three words:
>
> **For My Book**
>
> You are asking permission to record their experiences, knowledge and passion in a permanent medium ... a book.

All you need to change is the last word "book" to another reason to interview them.

Let's look at some possibilities:

1. Blog
2. Article
3. Podcast

4. Research Project
5. School Project

All these revised reasons for an interview are shorter term, smaller missions than writing a book.

Any of these "reasons to interview" can be set up in a few minutes to less than a day. There really is no excuse to let anything get in your way.

Let's take a look at each of them, see how to implement it and identify some of the pros and cons of each.

Blog

You've almost surely heard of blogging. The origin of the term comes from "web log" which was shortened to just "blog." It's just as the name implies, a log or a journal that people would keep on a website.

It has obviously grown to be much more than that now. There are many professional bloggers who earn a significant (six figures and more) income from business generated as a direct product or by-product of their blog.

There are many blogging platforms out there that are either hosted for you or where you can use your own domain name. Since the focus of this section is on being quick and easy, here are some of the top sites to look at for hosting your blog:

Wordpress.com

Blogger.com

Tumblr.com (not a typo)

Medium.com

Typepad.com

Weebly.com

Wix.com

All these sites can be set up at no cost and you will be on your way. Just follow the instructions on each site.

> **Pros:** Easy, quick and cheap to get started. Most people have heard of a blog, so it will be easy to get your interviewees to understand what you're doing
>
> **Cons:** Blogs have a reputation for being cheap and of poor quality since just about anyone can start one. Your guest may need some extra convincing about what you're doing and why he/she should participate.

A good alternative to get credibility and exposure would be to find an existing blog with readership and ask to be a guest blogger for that site. That way it will be an established brand you are representing when you go speak to your interviewees.

Article

This is another, even more obvious, reason to interview someone. There are articles in newspapers and magazines both online and offline. Just find a place that fits your goals and ask the publisher if you could write a guest article. A series of articles would be even better.

Depending on what you find, your articles could be seen as a huge benefit to your guests.

Pros: Easy and cheap to get started. It will have a higher perceived value than a blog to your guests because of readership reach and credibility.

Cons: Could be harder to find willing publishers to accept your work and it could take longer for your work to be published, as it needs to fit in with their scheduled release dates.

Podcast

Podcasts have been around since the 1980s as a way of audio-blogging or creating other audio content. When the iPod first became popular, there was then a great hardware platform for the podcasts to play on and Apple was a leading proponent for them.

There are now thousands of podcasts available from dozens of producers and directories. Apple's' iTunes is still the king, but there are other big ones like Stitcher and Soundcloud.

Pros: It's very easy to set up a podcast and there are many places that will host it and help you get a listenership. If you do an interview type podcast (which is of course what this is all about) your interviewees create the content for you.

Cons: Podcasts have been around for many years and gaining popularity at an exponential rate. But there are still a lot of people that don't know what they are. Therefore, it may be a bit harder to educate and to convince people to be on your podcast depending upon how tech savvy your field is.

Research Project

I left this one a bit open-ended. You need to decide what research you're doing and why. It needs to tie into your bigger picture goals. It could be something as simple as researching a new career and talking to people to find out more information about what it's all about.

It could be something much more in-depth and focused on a smaller topic area and discussing ideas with thought-leaders in your field about it. Just make it something that relates to your career and that It's something meaningful to you.

> **Pros:** You can pick virtually any topic or reason for the interview.

> **Cons:** It could be more unclear what you are doing and what the objectives are, unless you spend some time explaining your reasons for the project.

School Project

If you are still in school, you may have latitude to determine your own projects in certain classes. See if you can steer it toward something that will help your career. You may even approach a professor to see if he or she would sponsor you for some extra-curricular research in an area that they are interested in.

> **Pros:** Business people love to help students. It is a way for them to "give back" or even to invest

in future talent for their business, which is exactly what you want, too.

Cons: It requires a little cooperation from your school or sponsor, and you may be a little more constrained in what you want your focus and timeline to be.

Look over the possibilities I gave you for reasons to interview people. You can probably come up with even more or find better ways to use the ones I gave you. The point is that there are a lot of ways to get to talk to influential people if you look for them.

Pick one and move forward!

Pick your method, pick your topic and pick your "why." Then find the people who can help you with your blog, article, podcast or other project. It will be easy to get all of this set up, find the people you want to talk to and do it in less than seven days.

About the Author

"A positive attitude may not solve all your problems, but it will annoy enough people to make it worth the effort."

Herm Albright
German painter and lithographer

I grew up in the Atlanta, Georgia area. I lived in several areas around town, but I was in Red Oak throughout high school years, so that seems most like my hometown to me.

I was a very shy, introverted youth. I was literally scared as I walked down the street that someone might say "hi" to me … then I'd be on the spot to reply. It's taken me a lot of time and effort to overcome even these small hurdles.

I found that I was very good in math, but didn't have the funds to go to college out of state, so I looked into local schools to see what options I had for higher education.

It seemed that Georgia State, Georgia Tech or a local community college were my choices. Georgia Tech meant engineering and engineers needed to be good in math. I was good in math, therefore I would become an engineer. That's the extent of my thought

The Reverse Interview

process into what would become my career for many years. It seems so simplistic now that I look back at it, but at the same time it was so brilliant that I didn't complicate the matter.

I was good at math because I liked it and I went into a profession that used something that I liked. Does it need to get any more complicated than this?

What I learned later is that engineers tend to be good at sitting in a lab and working on "things" rather than interacting with people. Given my shy nature, that worked out just fine for me too.

Then I left the design world and decided to get into sales ... the absolute *last* thing I ever wanted to do when I graduated as an electrical engineer. Little did I know then that I would love it. Not for the sales part of it, but because I got to see some really cool things going on in the design of everything from medical instruments to steel mills, aircraft, automobiles, spacecraft, water testing, chicken farming and everything in between.

The part that took some getting used to was standing up in front of groups of up to two hundred people and giving presentations ... usually technical presentations about computer hardware and software designed for scientists and engineers. I also had to schedule at least sixteen meetings per week across a six-state area.

Being shy, I got very good at asking questions and listening. I was always in a learning mode instead of taking a salesy "pitch-man" approach.

Listening is a key ingredient to connecting

I never knew how few people were good at listening or how much it meant to people to be listened to. It was a great combination that led to becoming a top sales person. People liked me because I listened, I learned what they cared about, and then I gave them a solution to their concerns. Bazinga (my nerdy homage to the "Big Bang Theory" TV show)!

I sold millions of dollars' worth of stuff by listening and offering solutions and never once letting my desire to "make money" enter into the equation. It was always all about helping other people.

Now why am I writing about all of this? Because getting a job is a sales job no matter what kind of job you're looking for.

Be yourself.

Be a good listener.

Help other people.

I wrote this book because I was tired of hearing about people who are out of a job and have given up. There are always positions open for good people who care about others. Remember two of my favorite truisms:

"No one cares how much you know unless they know how much you care."

And

"In order to have everything you want in life, all you have to do is help enough other people get what they want."

This book is a precise, step-by-step manual to connect with people and show them how much you care. By helping others, you'll have all you want.

Charles

PS: I wish you nothing but success, happiness and a career that rewards you in every possible way.

Reverse Interview
"Quick Start" Certificate

For a limited time purchasers of this book may have access to additional video training

Visit:
ReverseInterview.com/special
Or Scan this QR Code:

Made in the USA
Charleston, SC
22 May 2015